William Powell James

Romantic Professions and other Papers

William Powell James

Romantic Professions and other Papers

ISBN/EAN: 9783744776707

Printed in Europe, USA, Canada, Australia, Japan

Cover: Foto ©Thomas Meinert / pixelio.de

More available books at **www.hansebooks.com**

ROMANTIC
PROFESSIONS
AND OTHER PAPERS

ROMANTIC PROFESSIONS

AND OTHER PAPERS
BY
W. P. JAMES

LONDON · ELKIN MATHEWS & JOHN LANE
AT THE SIGN OF THE BODLEY HEAD
NEW YORK · MACMILLAN & COMP? 1894 ·

Edinburgh: T. and A. CONSTABLE, Printers to Her Majesty

TO

F. B.

The following papers are reprinted, with revision, one from *Blackwood's Magazine*, and the others from *Macmillan's Magazine*, with the kind permission of the respective proprietors

CONTENTS

b

ROMANTIC PROFESSIONS

AN American moralist not long ago complained that the American girl, perverted by the reading of fairy tales in her childhood, turned up her pretty nose at the dry-goodsman of her native land and fed her romantic fancy with dreams of English dukes. This, if true, is beyond question deplorable. And yet I imagine that no fair-minded dry-goodsman with a competent knowledge of romantic literature would seriously propose himself, in his character of dry-goodsman, as a fitting hero for a maiden's dreams. Ignorant Briton that I am, I have only the vaguest notion of what the dry-goods business consists in, but I feel pretty confident that the records of authoritative romance might be searched in vain for a precedent. The American moralist must not however run away with the idea that herein this respectable profession labours under an exceptional disability, or that his

A   I

countrywomen indulge a more fastidious fancy than their sisters in less democratic lands. It is lamentable, indeed, when you come to reflect on it, how large a proportion of useful and respectable callings falls under the ban of romance. What poet or romancer ever made his first lover, for example, a bailiff or a beadle? Yet bailiffs and beadles are men and brothers. They may do their often-times dangerous duty with the dash of a Rupert or the cool courage of a Cromwell, yet they are frankly impossible as heroes of romance. De Quincey makes a remark somewhere to the effect that one would not be inclined to think highly of a man who, in the absence of predisposing circumstances, deliberately and for the love of the business decided to be a butcher. Yet butchers are husbands and fathers, and have blood in their veins as well as on their aprons. As a matter of statistics, I suppose hardly a day passes but some solicitor falls in love; yet no court of love or literature will give him audience as a lover, or take cognisance of his pleadings. The breast of the stockbroker is swayed by the bears and bulls of passion, no less than by the subtler influences of financial speculation. Yet his name is not honoured in the more than royal exchange of romance. Then, with one stroke of the pen, romance rules out the whole amorous mob of retail traders.

They are not altogether absent from the pages of romance, these worthy citizens. Only they have to forego the heroic parts, and put up with being supernumeraries or villains or comic characters. About the butcher I am doubtful. Not even Dickens, I think, found room for a butcher amid his Babylon of trades. A bailiff he has and eight sheriff's officers, half-a-dozen beadles, and half as many more brokers. The sheriff's officer is of course a familiar enough figure from the days of our literary drama. An ingenious American has compiled a list of Dickens's characters, classified by callings, and it reads like nothing so much as a trades' directory. There are architects, auctioneers, bankers, barbers, boarding-house keepers blacksmiths, carpenters, carriers, chandlers, chemists, clerks (a perfect army of them), coachmen, coal-merchants, constables, corn-chandlers, costumiers, detectives, doctors, domestic servants, dry-salters, engineers, engine-drivers, farmers, fishermen, game-keepers, grocers, greengrocers, haberdashers, hop-growers, jailers and turnkeys, labourers, lamplighters, lawyers, law-stationers, lock-smiths, manufacturers, merchants, medical students, money-lenders, notaries, ostlers, pawnbrokers, parish-clerks, plasterers, por-ters, post-masters, pot-boys, reporters, robe-makers, saddlers, sailors, sextons, shipwrights, stewards, stokers, stonemasons, sugar-bakers, tailors, teachers, tobacconists, toy-makers and merchants, umbrella-makers, undertakers, watermen, weavers, wharfingers, wheelwrights. The list might be made longer, but that perhaps is long enough to make you realise how amply provided with trades and tradesmen are the teeming streets of Dickens's imagination. And where in all the crowd is your hero of romance? Barkis, the carrier, no doubt, was willing, but it takes more than willingness to make the ideal lover. Nor did Dickens content himself with the ordinary trades. He loved to collect speci-mens of bizarre callings. There is Jo the crossing-sweeper, and Wegg the ballad-monger, and Boffin the dustman; he has a hangman and a resurrection-man; he has two balloonists, a bird-fancier, and a begging-letter writer; an astrologer and a pugilist,— Mr. Toots's friend the Game Chicken; dancing-masters, jugglers, cheap-jacks, show-men with a giant and a dwarf and a kept poet, a verger and a pew-opener, a stenographer and a statistician, a shoe-binder and a maker of nautical instruments; nor let me by any means forget Mr. Venus, articulator of bones. 'You're casting your eye round the shop, Mr. Wegg. Let me show you a light. My working-bench. My young man's bench. A wice. Tools. Bones, warious. Skulls, warious. Preserved Indian baby. African ditto. Bottled preparations, warious. Everything within reach of your hand, in good preser-vation. The mouldy ones atop.' Mr. Venus, it is true, as became his mythological name, had his little romance with Rogue Rider-hood's daughter. Now Pleasant Riderhood had no call to be squeamish. She was meagre and of muddy complexion, looked twice her age, and had a swivel eye. Yet even this apology for a girl had the hardihood to cast the good man's calling in his teeth, intimating that she neither regarded herself, nor wished to be regarded, in a bony light.

Another out-of-the-way trade in the same novel, and a prettier fancy, is that of Jenny Wren, the dolls' dressmaker. When Charley Hexam and Bradley Headstone called at Jenny Wren's house to look for Hexam's sister Lizzie, the quaint little 'person of the house' put them to guess the name of her trade and they had to give it up. Who but Dickens, indeed, would ever have thought of such a trade? Who but Dickens, did I say? Why, by an uncommonly curious coincidence M. Alphonse Daudet did actually hit upon precisely the same pretty fancy, for his Désirée Delobelle. He had been especially particular about a trade for her. She was the daughter of an actor ; and he determined that the theatricality of the father should in the crippled girl take the form of sentimental reverie, and that she must have some pretty and poetical business suggesting a luxury in contrast with her own poor surroundings. Dolls' dressmaking, the very thing! Poor and deformed herself, she could gratify her natural tastes for refinement and elegance, and dress her dreams instead of herself in silks and gold lace. It was M. Daudet's custom to compose his novels out loud, and he told André Gill one day about his little dolls' dressmaker. From him he learnt for the first time to his great dismay that there was already a dolls' dressmaker known to the world of fiction in a novel by Dickens, which M. Daudet happened not to know. The parallel was exact, the conception was the same and had been carried out with all the English novelist's sympathy with the poor, with all his *féerie de la rue*. M. Daudet knew that he had often before this been likened to Dickens, before he had read a line of him, and long before he had been told by a friend who had been in England that David Copperfield took a friendly interest in *Le Petit Chose*. He had much the same early experiences as Dickens, and shared his sympathy with the poor and wretched. Save so far as this community of experience and sympathy explained it, the coincidence about the dolls' dressmaker was pure chance. He recognised, however, that he would have to sacrifice his specially selected trade. How find another so ideally suitable,—*aussi poétiquement chimérique?* He felt with Balzac that such things could not be evolved out of a writer's inner consciousness. So he did what Balzac and Dickens often did in the like cases. He roamed the streets with his eyes open and climbed many a dark and dank staircase. At last he was rewarded. He saw a sign whose inscription dazzled him, faded though the gold letters were, *Oiseaux et mouches pour modes.* And a trade had been found, fairy-like and fantastic enough for *pauv' petite Mam'zelle Zizi.*

Balzac's *Comédie Humaine* teems like the world of Dickens with all sorts and conditions of men. A *répertoire* compiled by two pious and industrious Balzaciens takes between five and six hundred ample French octavo pages merely to enumerate his characters with the briefest possible description of them. From this source the curious might readily lengthen Dickens's extensive

and peculiar list, and add thereto some unsavoury trades. But I have digressed too
long, tempted by the pleasures of wandering
in the by-ways of romance. I was looking
for the ideal lover, and among all these
curious crowds I find him not. Nor with
Shakespeare is it any better. Quince the
carpenter, Snug the joiner, Bottom the
weaver, Flute the bellows-mender, Snout
the tinker, and Starveling the tailor, are all
very well to play the fool, to divert the
duke and the ladies, but none of them, not
even Bottom translated, is a fit object for a
lady's love. As the democratic Whitman
has complained, in a Shakespearian play the
mass of industrious citizens is just a mob
to throw up its sweaty night-caps in some
Cæsar's honour at the bidding of an Antony.
What is there about a trade thus to incapa-
citate a man for romance?

Strictly speaking, there are but two
normal heroes of romance, the warrior and
the fairy prince. If there is no fairy prince
at hand, an ordinary prince will do. The
English duke is, as the American moralist
rightly enough divined, only a modern

variety of fairy prince. To be mistaken
for a fairy prince the English duke no
doubt needs to be looked at from the other
side of the Atlantic. Seen at close quarters,
in the House of Lords, on the race-course,
or in the law-courts, he is apt to appear
fleshy. But he has the essential attribute
of the fairy prince, which is rarity. There
are but two dozen or so of him all told,
and most of these have been bespoken or
used up. He has besides, for the American
girl, another of the essential secrets of
romance; he is exotic. It is the good
fortune and fascinating fashion of the fairy
prince to descend always from some unknown upper and diviner air. That it is
which makes the Prince Charming of the
fairy tale so irresistible. So it was that
Cupid came to Psyche, to cherish her with
his secret and invisible godhead. So Perseus
floated on winged sandals through the wel-
coming air to Andromeda's feet, to slay the
monster. So Lohengrin came flashing in a
swan-drawn skiff from the mysterious halls
of the Holy Grail, to champion maiden
innocence against treachery and slander.

The fairy prince, you see, commonly includes the warrior's part, and is doubly resistless coming in the nick to fight a distressed damsel's battles and to slay her dragons. Another good plan is to come in a shower of gold, as Zeus came to Perseus's mother. The charm of strangeness, however, and of unlooked-for arrival, is mighty of itself; it is potent with princes and princesses as with humbler folk. You may recall the case of Prince Camaralzaman and Princess Badoura. In spite of his father's wishes and entreaties, Prince Camaralzaman was obstinately set against matrimony. Seeing no one to his fancy about him, he inveighed, as man will, against the whole sex. He told his match-making old father that the mischief which history taught him women had caused in the world, and the accounts he daily heard to their disadvantage, powerfully influenced him, so that he was more and more confirmed in his resolution not to marry. By way of retort, the king very properly shut him up in a tower on short commons for his contumacy and cynicism. Meanwhile in far off China the

Princess Badoura was likewise in durance, for being no less wilfully set against the slit-eyed suitors she pictured to her imagination from the celestial specimen which had fallen under her observation. Well, no sooner had the fairy Maimoune and the genie Danhasch, to decide a private wager of their own, whisked this precious couple through the air into each other's presence, than lo! these hardened celibates were afire in a twinkling.

You may depend upon it that what tells chiefly with the girls against the eminently respectable race of bankers and brewers and doctors and lawyers is their appalling commonness, their frequency, I mean, and familiarness. What should there be in one brass plate out of a dozen in the same street to throw a romantic girl off her emotional balance? So far as Miss Rosamond Vincy could be described as thrown off her emotional balance, the charm that subdued her was not Lydgate's fine professional enthusiasm, but the descent of a stranger and gentleman into the mediocrity of Middlemarch. He was for Rosamond the prince of the fairy stories. His devotion to science, and his connection with Bulstrode's hospital, were humiliations to be endured for a season. And so you will often find it. When the modern novelist would surmount the professional high hat with the aureole of romance, he tricks out his tame hero to mimic the traditional advantages of prince or champion.

Of the warrior as hero, what need of argument? His praise is in all the churches of orthodox romance. From the heroes of Troy down to Ouida's Guardsmen and Mr. Kipling's Musketeers, he simply dominates the record. History (it is the bitter cry of the scientific historian) has been but the gallery of his triumphs and trophies. The epic was invented to do him honour. Throughout the romances proper, of Roland and Richard, of the Round Table and the Romancero, he reigns without a rival. In the Sagas his pre-eminence is, if possible, even more pronounced. These be documents, no doubt, of fighting epochs. Yet the sentiment is the same in the sovereign cycle of modern romance, the Waverley

Novels, the author whereof was bred a lawyer in a literary and civilised city. Sir Walter did not set great store by his heroes, but such as they are, they are all good men of their hands. They are either soldiers, or gentlemen at large ready to strike a blow for liege or lady. Personally he felt more enthusiasm about the creation of Bailie Nicol Jarvie; but he did not expect the girls to take the same view. Apparent exceptions, like Frank Osbaldistone or Darsie Latimer, do but prove the rule. There is no more of the lawyer about the one than there is of the merchant about the other. They are simply spirited young gentlemen with the knack for getting on the track of an adventure, the one real business after all of a hero of romance. Roland Graeme of *The Abbot*, by the way, reminds one of another traditional type of hero of romance : my lady's page, who for mediæval reasons plays a pretty part in mediæval romance.

Scott was a man of letters and a lawyer, but the imaginative Clerk of Session had the blood of the fighting Borderers in his

veins, and was prouder of that than of his
legal or his literary status. He was a
soldier at heart; he would have loved to
be a soldier indeed; he flung himself into
volunteering when the Frenchman loomed
large on the national apprehension; so soon
as he had a son to serve, he made a soldier
of him. Yet he does not need this traditional taste in Scott's own case to explain
the predilection of the romancer in him for
soldier heroes. It is the general sentiment.
The soldier is the natural hero. In a recent
book of Chinese stories, Professor Douglas
contrasts the Chinese sentiment in this
matter with the rest of the world's. Military
prowess, he says, does not attract popular
applause in China. In the eyes of the
Chinese, a man is a model hero who takes
the highest degrees at the examinations
and quotes the classics with the greatest
fluency. The rest of the world thinks differently. Even the cynical youngster whom
Woolwich or Sandhurst sends forth to pro-
vide the dark places of the provinces with
polo matches and private theatricals, shines
with some of the reflected glory of Achilles

and Lancelot. Besides the glory of tradition, there is moreover the glory of the uniform. The influence of a uniform in romance is beyond gainsaying. The effect of a red coat on susceptible hearts below stairs is accounted by the most unsentimental critics an effective ally of the recruiting sergeant. It is perhaps, as Sir Lucius O'Trigger surmised, a bit of the old serpent in the women that makes the little creatures be caught like vipers with a piece of red cloth. But there is a deeper reason. The ideal soldier is the ideal man. To be ever a fighter, as Browning boasted, is it not after all man's destiny and function? The eighteenth is not accounted one of the most romantic centuries, nor was Samuel Johnson its most feather-headed thinker; yet this is what he thought of soldiers.

'*Johnson*: Every man thinks meanly of ' himself for not having been a soldier, or ' not having been at sea. *Boswell*: Lord ' Mansfield does not. *Johnson*: Sir, if ' Lord Mansfield were in a company ' of General Officers and Admirals, who ' have been in service, he would shrink;

'he'd wish to creep under the table. *Boswell*:
'No; he'd think he could try them all.
'*Johnson*: Yes, if he could catch them; but
'they'd try him much sooner. No, sir;
'were Socrates and Charles the Twelfth of
'Sweden both present in any company, and
'Socrates to say, "Follow me, and hear a
'lecture in Philosophy;" and Charles, laying
'his hand on a sword, to say "Follow me
'and dethrone the Czar," a man would be
'ashamed to follow Socrates. Sir, the im-
'pression is universal. Sir, the profession
'of soldiers and sailors has the dignity of
'danger. Mankind reverence those who
'have got over fear, which is so general a
'weakness.'

The great doctor was right. Courage is
at the root of all worth. The late Edward
Fitzgerald, a literary hermit of great discernment, was fond of insisting on the un-
diminished need for physical prowess and
the barbaric virtues in advanced and refined
stages of civilisation. A woman is right in
demanding in her hero a stout heart and a
strong arm,—strength, courage and loyalty,
the soldier's virtues.

Johnson couples the sailor with the soldier, and who shall deny the sailor's place in romance? Not the Englishman surely, the islander, the descendant of Vikings and of Elizabeth's sea-dogs, the countryman of Drake and Nelson and the men of the little *Revenge.* In fiction, too, the sailor has a whole province to himself from Marryat to Mr. Clark Russell, and a dynasty of heroes from noble Amyas Leigh to the queer crew of *The Wrecker.* Literature has little to add to the picturesqueness, the natural poetry and romance of their calling who go down to the sea in ships and exercise their business in great waters. The sea itself has been a passion with poets from Æschylus to Mr. Swinburne. There are ballads, too, of the lass that loved a sailor, and a lax tradition gives Jack a wife in every port,— a privilege which the latest romancer among the French Immortals has illustrated with a licence of exotic grace which does more credit to his æsthetic than his moral sensibility. And yet, for all this, the sailor is no real rival for the soldier in romance. The sailor is a hero for a romance of adventure,

excellent among icebergs or pirates or on a
treasure-hunt. He is a sort of specialist in
romance. Whereas the ideal soldier is, as I
have said, simply the ideal man. One may
perhaps venture to say so now that the
tyranny of Cobdenism is overpast. An era
of economic industrialism was mightily
shocked at the barbarism of the soldier,
and the brutality of war. Tennyson's fierce
denunciation of the canker of ignoble peace
was treated as an outbreak of hysteria.
Wordsworth's uncompromising salutation of
Carnage as 'God's daughter' was decided to
be the blasphemy against the Holy Ghost.
Well, we have had industrial wars since then ;
which seem to have all the cruelty and none
of the heroism of old-fashioned warfare.

Is not this the explanation of the incon-
gruousness of most trades and professions
for a hero? Is it not because there is
something essentially dehumanising about
this minute division of labour, on which
economic civilisation prides itself? Rogue
Riderhood's daughter was right ; her taunt
was fair. What a girl wants is a man, not
an articulator of bones, nor even, for the

matter of that, a man of law or medicine.
A professional man is a subdivided man or
a warped man ; a man with a crease in him,
as the French say. And it is just this
warping which makes him unmeet for a
hero, and at the same time so useful on the
stage of a Balzac or a Dickens. It adds the
grotesque and bizarre touch, affords piquant
contrasts, supplies a characteristic chorus.
Shakespeare uses such effects, the juxta-
position for example of the pessimism of
the apothecary with the passion of Romeo,
Hamlet's metaphysical horror of death, and
the grave-digger that had so little feeling of
his business that he sang at grave-making,
custom having made it in him, as Horatio
explained, a property of easiness. We have
noted an example of the dramatic value of
a *métier* in Dickens's dolls' dressmaker, and
M. Daudet's substitute, the making-up of
artificial birds. Trades and professions
have, many of them, such traditional dramatic values ; the professional gloom of the
undertaker, the glibness of the auctioneer,
the astuteness of the lawyer. It is a wonder,
in this age of laborious and methodical

fiction, that no one has projected a series
of novels to exploit the dramatic possibilities
of the various callings after an encyclopædic
fashion. It would have been a task worthy
of M. Zola's solid perseverance. Flaubert
did propose to devote a novel to Monsieur
le Préfet, affirming that nobody had fully
grasped how comical, how self-important, and
how useless a character a préfet was. Balzac
in fact made considerable contributions : *Le
Médecin de Campagne*, *Le Curé de Village*,
Scènes de la Vie Militaire, *Scènes de la Vie
Politique*. What titanic tradesmen he would
have given us, had he set his mind to it!

When I hinted that nine out of ten men
sold their birthright of romance for a mess
of pottage when they made choice of a
respectable profession, I used the word
'respectable' advisedly. For if your calling
be the exact opposite of respectable there
is no difficulty whatever about your figuring
as a hero. Rogues and vagabonds, adven-
turers, outlaws, smugglers, highwaymen and
pirates have ever been dear to romance.
The 'picaresque' novel is one of the largest
and most ancient kinds. It may be said to

have begun with the very beginning of prose fiction, with that most delightful of books, the *Golden Ass* of Apuleius, and with the *Satyricon* of Petronius, whose indescribable filth is redeemed by undeniable genius. Nash's *Unfortunate Traveller*, Jack Wilton, was an arrant scamp, a true forerunner of the Captain Carletons and Jonathan Wilds, whose legitimate rank nobody denies. Jack Sheppard and Claud Duval have vied in popular vogue with any knight-errant of them all; so has Robin Hood, who no doubt was a bit of a socialist and carried on his depredations on sentimental principles. The successful trickster has been a favourite in fiction from Ulysses to Brer Rabbit. Gil Blas was a rogue and a vagabond if ever there was one, and no hero in fiction has a more esteemed following. Le Sage is the direct ancestor of Fielding and Smollett, and Joseph Andrews, like Gil Blas, was a lacquey, at first blush you would say the most unheroic of parts.

If a would-be hero have not the mental qualifications for playing the rogue, it is an excellent plan for him to be a foundling like

Tom Jones, or to get cruelly changed at birth, a seeming mischance that has made the romantic fortunes of hundreds of heroes. Another good plan is to turn strolling player; the status of rogue and vagabond has indeed been conferred on strolling and unlicensed players by statute. The high rank of the strolling player in modern fiction dates at least as far back as the 'Roman Comique.' Scarron's Destin is the acknowledged first parent of Gautier's Capitaine Fracasse, and the family includes various specimens from the harmless Nicholas Nickleby to the didactic and unwholesome Wilhelm Meister.

The criminal, or semi-criminal, hero suggests his natural enemy the detective hero—also a very popular class. The police novel is as distinct a kind as the picaresque. The great Gaboriau has been reported to be Prince Bismarck's favourite reading; like another Greek he conquered his country's conqueror. The illustrious Lecoq of Gaboriau and Boisgobey is no more, but I am told that Sherlock Holmes is a worthy successor. And before Lecoq there were In-

spector Bucket and the amateur detectives of
Poe's mysteries. The tracking of a criminal
mystery, like the quest of a hidden treasure,
is a staple motive in romance. It was a
strong element in Dickens, as the authors of
The Wreckers say they found after starting
independently on analogous lines. It was
the all in all, or nearly all, with his friend
Wilkie Collins. But the great parent of the
police-novel, as of so much else, was Balzac.
The death-struggle of the criminal classes
under Vautrin against the police (under
Bibi-Lupin, wasn't it?) is epic in its scale
and tragic in its painfulness.

There is certainly something unheroic
about respectability. Lord Brabourne has
expressed the opinion (and it is reassuring to
have the countenance of even a newly-created
peer when one goes about to impugn so respectable a British institution as respectability)
that Emma's middle-aged Knightley was
altogether too respectable for a hero. Three
of her heroes, indeed, Miss Austen made not
only respectable but reverend, which is respectability carried to a higher power. The
professional respectability of her clerical

lovers was, however, tempered by advantages of worldly position. Edward Ferrars, Henry Tilney, and Edmund Bertram were heirs to titles or properties. The parson in the popular fiction of the last century was neither specially hampered by respectability nor made romantic by position. His fore-ordained fate was the lady's maid. In spite of his comparative popularity with novelists, there is in fiction something uncomfortable about the clerical lover. It may be a sur-vival of a sentiment engendered by a celibate priesthood. In George Eliot's *Scenes of Clerical Life* Captain Wybrow was the most unheroic of military heroes, yet most girls would have made Tina's mistake of pre-ferring that barber's block to the good-natured Gilfil. As for poor Amos Barton, he is not in the romantic running. Even in Barchester, where the very air you breathe is clerical, and the babies must have been born shovel-hatted, one has this uncomfort-able feeling. Among Mary Bold's lovers the outrageous Bertie Stanhope is a relief by contrast with his clerical rivals, the too academic Arabin and the unspeakable Slope.

The disability extends beyond the strict bounds of clericalism. I doubt whether Jan Ridd had the right to make Lorna Doone end her romantic days as the wife of a churchwarden. In spite of Charlotte Brontë, the *Professor* smacks something too much of edification—Charlotte Brontë was governess to the marrow, and looked at life through the governess's spectacles. The schoolmaster's is almost inevitably an invidious *rôle*. He is born to the disdain of your Steerforths and Guy Livingstones, who cannot carry their condescension further than to flirt with his wife. If he is a villain he is as villainous as Bradley Headstone. If he is a hero, his temporary position as usher is undeniably derogatory. Think of Le Petit Chose. Think of Nicholas Nickleby ; not the company of Fanny Squeers and Tilda Price could make his lot romantic. Things are better in America. To be 'the master' of such native daughters of the West as Mr. Bret Harte's Mliss and Cressy cannot be described as a position otherwise than exciting. And, thanks to the snake's spell of Elsie Venner, Mr. Bernard Langdon could not complain of dulness at the Apollinean Female Institute of Rockland.

The only way to work the clerical hero is to exalt him into a saint or to depress him into a sinner. The last is the more feasible plan. It lends itself better to the essential element of the eternal feminine. That was Hawthorne's way in *The Scarlet Letter* (a way that has of late been imitated more than once by lady novelists), and the Reverend Arthur Dimmesdale is a romantic success of the first water. The saint, the missionary, the martyr is a type of hero than which none is finer, only he is a bit unmanageable as a lover. There are other types of parsons in fiction ; but it is not as a lover that one loves Dr. Primrose, or Parson Adams, nor was the Reverend Charles Honeyman ever reckoned a hero of romance.

Another rather interesting point to observe is the contrast, in respect of susceptibility of romantic treatment, between what I may call the trades and professions of the town and the simpler country crafts. The plough-boy is perfectly at his case in poetry, whereas, as some critic has complained, a

hatter is unmentionable in serious verse.
The shepherd, the hunter, the fisherman, the
miller, the village blacksmith, and their various pursuits are of the very stuff and sub-
stance of poetry from the dawn of literature;
and they are as picturesque as ever to-day in
the village idylls of George Sand or in the
boasted realism of Mr. Hardy. About the
plumber, on the other hand, in spite of his
malignant power, there is an intensity of
prose that baffles the transfiguring power of
genius. Your over-civilised *grand siècle* tries
to get a whiff of poetry out of sham shepherd-
ing in court pastorals. But courtiers never
played at plumbers, nor masqueraded as
manufacturers. This element of irreducible
prose in modern life has been a difficulty
with artists and poets, and various ways
have been tried of getting over it. They
reduce themselves chiefly to Tennyson's way
and Walt Whitman's. Tennyson's was essentially the device of poetic diction against
which Wordsworth waged a victorious war,
though it must be confessed that many a
creeping line of his has since died of its
wounds. Mr. Churton Collins, in his rather

deplorable little book on Tennyson, has denounced it as a presenting of perfectly commonplace things in a euphuism that bordered on the ludicrous. Only one asks, why is the hatter commonplace, while the miller is romantic ? Why is the miller's daughter in every poet's mouth, while the hatter's daughter blooms unsung ? A bailiff's daughter, by the way, has been beatified in a ballad. Well, Walt Whitman, as became the poet of democracy, did not admit the distinction. He faced the difficulty with his customary uncalculating courage. He wrote a poem directly in point for my present purpose, calling it *A Carol of Occupations.* Here are some of the lines—

Leather-dressing, coach-making, boiler-making, rope-twisting.

Distilling, sign-painting, lime-burning, cotton-picking, Electro-plating, electro-typing, stereotyping.

The implements for daguerreotyping, the tools of the rigger, grappler, sail-maker, block-maker.

Goods of gutta-percha, *papier-maché*, colours, brushes, brush-making, glaziers' implements.

The veneer and gluepot, the confectioners' ornaments, the decanter and glass, the shears and flat iron.

Or again—

Beef on the butcher's stall, the slaughter-house of the butcher, the butcher in his killing-clothes.

The pens of live pork, the killing-hammer, the hog-
    hook,
The scalder's tub, gutting, the cutler's cleaver, the
    packer's maul,
And the plenteous winter-work of pork-packing.

About which all I will say is this, that we
don't call it 'carolling' in the old country.
Electro-plating and pork-packing may be
the last refinements of American civilisation,
but they certainly lack the old-fashioned
flavour of romance. This difference of poetic
and prosaic callings is indubitable, explain
it how one may. Nor is it simply a matter
of old fashion and poetic tradition, for Mr.
Bret Harte's digger is as romantic as any
shepherd of them all, and so, for the matter
of that, is the illicit distiller of the Great
Smoky Mountain.

Of course, when the modern novelist
grasped the full seriousness of his high calling, when instead of a story he felt com-
pelled to offer a 'criticism of life,' when he
disdained to amuse and aspired to become
our spiritual Baedeker, when he took to pro-
pounding 'the pure woman' of the future, to
introducing the era of the New Chivalry, or
inculcating a divine discontent of things as

they are, and generally to reduplicating instead of lightening

> 'the heavy and the weary weight
> Of all this unintelligible world,'

he could no longer blink the prosaic parts of life.

The modern maiden, it has to be admitted, wants not merely a man, but a man who will make a decent living; and, after Balzac's minute preoccupation with ways and means, it has become impossible to leave a hero and a heroine with no visible means of subsistence but the empty air of romance. So if all the men were not to be represented in fiction as men of means like Miss Austen's lay lovers, the pampered race of Darcys, Bingleys, Willoughbys and the rest, the professional or trading hero became inevitable. I dare say that if a patient German critic could take a census of the unnumbered heroes of modern fiction, he might find heroes of all conditions, from an archbishop in his vestments to a butcher in his killing-clothes. I would still, however, hazard the conjecture that they would be found to be represented as heroes in spite of their various trades and professions rather than by virtue thereof. You cannot somehow sing a pæan over a well-drawn conveyance, or an achievement in painless dentistry, as you can over the smithying of Sigurd's sword.

There are, it is true, a few professions about which hangs some faint aroma of romance. There is the profession of politics to which Benjamin Disraeli devoted himself in fiction and fact. The diplomatist ranks high with a certain order of novelist. Ouida in one of her higher flights immortalised a Queen's messenger. The barrister, oddly enough, is a not uncommon hero. Is it the wig and robes, or the prospect (precarious, as Eugene Wrayburn's boy hinted to Mr. Boffin) of ending in the House of Peers? See, here again, how the conflict crops up between professionalism and romance. It is the briefless barrister who is the more generally accepted hero,—your Darsie Latimer or Arthur Pendennis. Mr. Stryver gets the briefs and pockets the fees; but it is Sydney Carton who plays the hero's part and lays down his life for his love. For one thing, your rising junior is generally bald, and romance abhors a bald head.

It is one of the grievances of what is invidiously called the lower branch of the legal profession, that while the briefless barrister is accepted for hero, the attorney is more commonly the villain of the piece. The attorney's record is so bad in fiction, that it would be little better than a bit of bravado to attempt to impose him as hero on a prejudiced public. I do not know whether the task has been attempted even by the modern realist with all his love for the unlovely things of life. It would be highly diverting, though hardly fair to a learned and honourable profession, to institute a sort of tug of war between the virtuous and vicious attorneys of fiction, the types of Glossin and Messrs. Dodson and Fogg do so painfully prevail. It adds a deeper discredit to Philip Wakem's deformity that he had in him an attorney's blood. The law itself does not alas! command affection. Mental subtlety is ever suspect. If a lawyer be not astute he is naught, and astuteness is a quality that is neither honoured, loved nor trusted. Dirk

Hatteraick was not a nice man for a tea-party ; but he carries the reader with him when he dashes out Glossin's hateful brains. The public has got it into its head that the attorney cannot lose the lawyer in the lover, but will, like the young man by the name of Guppy, file a declaration instead of making a proposal, and write his love-letters without prejudice.

The leech came off almost as badly as the lawyer in the early days of fiction. In Scarron, Molière, and Le Sage, the doctor is simply a quack and is made the butt of unceasing satire. Among his diverse rogueries Gil Blas was doctor for a bit, and did uncommonly well at it. He practised the system of his employer Sangrado. The system was uniform and simple. It consisted, whatever the malady, in bleeding the patient and making him drink hot water till he died. One day Gil Blas had the bad luck to find a rival doctor at a patient's bedside, a disbeliever in Sangrado's system. When his famous system was impeached Gil Blas lightly retorted that some doctors killed their patients with bleedings and hot water, and

others killed them without, and that was all
the difference. And then, instead of a con-
sultation, they came to fisticuffs. But the
medical hero has looked up of late. It is
one result of the modern prestige of physical
science. Some cynics hint that systems
bearing a strong family likeness to the system of Sangrado have their seasons of super-
stitious acceptance even in these enlightened
days. And quacks and impostors there are
still in modern fiction. There is, to take
but one example, the odious Dr. Jenkins
of M. Daudet's *Nabab*. But more commonly of late he is the good angel of the
story like the delightful old doctor in the
same author's *Jack*. They say that an English lady, having read about Bianchon in
Balzac, would have no other physician and
wrote directly to Paris for his address, and
no one who knows Bianchon will quarrel
with her discretion. The physician's is in
truth a noble profession, giving scope for the
highest in a man of head and heart. This
was George Eliot's ideal in Lydgate, the
scientific humanist in reality, not in Mr.
Meredith's satirical sense. Lydgate certainly

compares very favourably with the bucolic
Sir James and the pedant Casaubon, and
perhaps with the inconclusive Will,—though
that is not saying a great deal.

The last received into the ranks of romantic professions is journalism. Any tolerably
wide reader of modern fiction cannot fail to
have been struck with the new and wide-
spread fashion for the scribbling hero. Mr.
Bret Harte gave us for hero the other day a
young man, who had 'made the second
column of *The Clarion* famous.' We already
had Tom Towers of the *Jupiter* and Pendennis and Warrington ; not that Pen was particularly heroic, in truth hardly more heroic
than the great F. B., another light of the
periodical press—nor half so lovable. Mr.
Edmund Yates has recorded the excitement
and delight with which the young Bohemian
writers of his day found their class for the
first time truly depicted in pages destined to
become immortal. Nor again will any one
be likely to forget the wonderful description
in *Les Illusions Perdues* of Lucien de
Rubempré's career as a journalist ; the un-
mistakable touch of early genius, its discovery

and exploiting by the harder heads around him, the sudden success and fame, then intrigues, temptations, and ⁺ degradation. It is the tragedy of journalism. These however were pioneers, and exceptional. The species has increased and multiplied mightily of late. We owe most examples perhaps to the American story. Next to prospecting and gambling, fighting in the war and travelling in Europe, being on the staff of a newspaper is the most romantic part for the American hero. They have become common enough among ourselves; it is surprising in how many recent novels they are to be found. If the young journalist is thereby tempted to believe himself a hero and to be puffed up, he may be recommended to re-read Mr. Gissing's *New Grub Street*, or to peruse Schopenhauer's or Mr. George Meredith's opinions of his profession.

The pretty oracle whereby young girls try their fortunes in plucking flower-petals recognises only seven classes of contingent lovers,—tinker, tailor, soldier, sailor, gentleman, ploughboy, thief. Soldiers, sailors, gentlemen, ploughboys, and thieves we have already admitted into the heroic hierarchy. There remain tinkers and tailors. I cannot think of a tinker, but two tailors occur at once to the mind, Alton Locke and Evan Harrington. Tradition has been hard on the tailor. The laugh has never died out against the three tailors of Tooley Street who began a petition with 'We the people of England.' And, in spite of the tailor-hero in the old German ballad who cut the devil's tail off, and that other who killed seven flies at one blow of his leathern flap and went a-knight-erranting with 'Seven at one blow' for his device, an ancient saw reckons nine tailors to a man. Nor, I fear, do my modern instances altogether do away the slur. When a Christian Socialist wrote what the Germans call a *Tendenzroman* against the sweating-system, he was almost forced to choose a tailor for hero. Yet even so, Kingsley did not venture to make him a tailor pure and simple. The most Christian of Socialists could not carry the courage of his convictions to that length. So he made Alton Locke a tailor-poet. Now poets have been licensed lovers time out of mind, since

Alain Chartier was paid for his poesy with a queen's kiss,—nay, since Apollo had all the nine Muses at his heels. And as for Evan Harrington, his is a leading case for the incompatibility of tailoring and romance. For see how Rose Jocelyn felt about it. Rose Jocelyn is one of the nicest girls in the galaxy of the girls of fiction. She was a lady in heart no less than by birth and breeding ; independent in character, fearless in judgment, free from petty prejudice. She had been long and intimately acquainted with Evan Harrington, and was thoroughly in love with him. She knew him to be worthy in all respects, and that no calling could make him other than a gentleman. Yet when the first hint of his being a tailor reached her, there was a sharp twitch in her body as if she had been stung or struck. And when her maid was undressing her at night and talked, as I suppose maids will, of their young ladies' young gentlemen, Rose started off by asking her what was the nick-name people gave to tailors, and was told they were called 'snips.' And Rose, standing sideways to the glass, repeated the word

to herself and then covered her face with her
hands and shuddered. And mind you, there
had been no warping in Evan's case. He
never was a tailor till his mother's rather
acrid probity made him one. He never sat
cross-legged in his life. No more for the
matter of that did the great Mel, the tailor,
his father. Mel was as little of a tailor as
might be, and was riding gallantly to hounds
while the shop was going steadily to the
dogs. It was admitted on all hands that
Mel was a man of heroic proportions. And
yet, because he was a tailor, the whole world
laughed at him.

No, so long as the guinea stamp means
so much even when the man is all gold, so
long as a man's soul seems thus to get a
smirch of trade on it, it is grievously to be
feared that even democratic damsels will
continue to prefer the duke to the dry-
goodsman.

THE NEMESIS OF SENTI-
MENTALISM.

SAINTE-BEUVE, it is well-known, signal-
ised *Madame Bovary* as the herald of a
new spirit in literature. Of this spirit he
thought he detected symptoms all around
him : science, the spirit of observation,
maturity, strength, a touch of hardness ;
' Anatomists and physiologists,' he concludes,
' I meet you on all sides.' That was thirty
years ago. The world has had enough and
to spare since then, in fiction and elsewhere,
of anatomy and physiology. Among other
manifestations, what Tennyson called Zolaism has gathered to a head. Flaubert is
still by many regarded as one of the high
priests of Zolaism, or rather perhaps as one
of the prophets to prepare the way for the
full revelation of Zolaism, who desired to

see the things that we see. M. Zola was a personal friend of Flaubert, and claimed for his own work the benefit of the prestige of Flaubert's name and fame. He has found Flaubert worthy of a place in the apostolical succession from Stendhal down to himself, the reigning pope.

Flaubert himself protested, so far as it lay in his proud and reserved nature to protest, against this enforced consecration. While recognising and encouraging the early promise of his younger friends, M. Zola, M. Daudet and the brothers Goncourt, he resented George Sand's labelling them as his 'school.' These friends of his, he pleaded, laboured for what he despised, and were at small pains about that which with himself was the object of tormenting search. The word is not a whit too strong for what Mr. Pater has called Flaubert's martyrdom for style. For himself, he regarded as of very secondary importance technical detail, local information, in short, the historical and literal aspect of things. His supreme aim was beauty, for which his fellow-workers displayed but scant zeal. It is interesting to know, and to know from his own lips, that he shared with Tourguéneff neither his severity towards 'Jack' nor the immensity of his admiration for 'Son Excellence Eugène Rougon': one, in his opinion, had charm, the other strength, but neither one nor other was mainly preoccupied with what for him was the end of art—with beauty. He muses rather sadly, how difficult it is for us to understand one another. Here were two men, whom he was very fond of, both, in his judgment, true artists— Tourguéneff and Zola. Yet all the same they in no wise admired Chateaubriand's prose, and still less Gautier's. They saw nothing in phrases which filled him with rapture.

In a word, then, so far from regarding himself as the founder of this new school, Flaubert in his own eyes was rather the last of the Romantics. In his letters to George Sand he was fond of calling himself *votre vieux romantique.* Hugo, Chateaubriand, Gautier were gods of his idolatry. He couples himself with Gautier as a survivor from an earlier age. In those sad days after

43

1870, Gautier in Paris, if still a god, was a god in exile. There were new religions in art. 'Poor Théo,' sighs Flaubert, 'no one now speaks his language. We are fossils stranded and out of place in a new world.' We find him again in those later years complaining that men of letters were so little men of letters in his sense. There was hardly any one save Hugo left, with whom he could talk of things that interested him. One day Hugo quoted to him some passages from Boileau and Tacitus; it was as if he had received a present, Flaubert said, so rare had the thing become.

Nevertheless, in spite of all this, Sainte-Beuve, being a looker on, perhaps in some sense saw best how the game was going. Flaubert had undeniably more in common with this new world than he would seem to have been himself aware. If he was a Romantic, his Romanticism was at all events not the Romanticism of 1830; he wore his red waistcoat with a very decided difference. There is more science, more observation, in a sense more maturity; there is none of the froth and exuberance of 1830.

But with the exuberance are gone also the
élan and the charm of youth of the early
Romantics. It is Romanticism grown old,
which has outlived not only the follies of
youth, but also its *insouciance*, its vigorous
spontaneousness, its faith and enthusiasm.
There was only one thing he wanted,
Flaubert said, but that was a thing not to
be had for the asking—an enthusiasm of
some sort. In playful seriousness, he signs
one letter *Directeur des Dames de la Désil-
lusion.* Disenchantment is the secret at
once of his bitterness and his force. If the
beautiful Aladdin's palace of romantic art
be only a phantom palace of magic, he will
steadfastly fix his disenchanted gaze on the
barren site, left more barren by the flight of
the past splendour. But his soul still yearns
for the beauty of it, and the old enchantment
has thus much sway over his imagination
still, that the remembered glory dwarfs and
makes drearier the natural landscape.

Disenchantment is the Nemesis of the
tricks which romance is apt to play with
fact. There is a beauty which includes fact,
which is beyond and above fact. That is

the sphere where Shakespeare dwells—not alone. But there is also a beauty which lies by the side of fact. The weaker impulse of romance is tempted sometimes to shrink from the roughness of the way and to turn aside into By-Path Meadow; and thereby fails to attain to the Beulah of poetic truth. Rightly enjoyed, By-Path Meadow need prove no primrose path to the everlasting bonfire. Like that other meadow which lay upon the banks of the river of water of life, the meadow beautiful with lilies and green all the year round, where Christian and Hopeful lay down and slept, its sunlit flowers may afford rest and recreation from the dust and heat of the main road of life. But those who mistake it for the highway may find themselves astray. Vain Confidence, seeking by this path the Celestial Gate, is apt to fall into the deep pit which is on purpose there made by the prince of these grounds to catch vain-glorious fools withal, and to be dashed to pieces by his fall. Some nobler souls the path may lead, as it led Christian and his companion, as it led Flaubert, to a sojourn in the dungeons of the Giant De-

spair. A strong Shakespeare absorbs and
supersedes the weaker romance, gives us
poetry, which is at once more real and more
romantic than the romances in vogue before
his day. Yet even Shakespeare, before
attaining to the ripe graciousness of Pros-
pero, had perhaps his fleeting mood of
Timon. And from his great contemporary
Cervantes the romances drew a spirit, which
was only not bitter irony, because it was
first of all pitying humour. In the case of
Flaubert the spirit of observation, married
to his early Romanticism, begot, alas! no
Shakespearian offspring, no radiant romance
of reality. The offspring is disillusion, with
bitter and mordant irony.

For all but the strongest natures the
romance which is primarily picturesque is a
delightful playground, but a bad school.
Naturally so, because it was never meant
for a school to learn the discipline of life in.
For the experienced, for the worker, for
the weary, romance is pure blessing. For
inexperience and youth the blessing is not
without its danger. Thus much foundation
at all events Plato had for the severity of

his famous judgment. After the glowing
colour and deep shadows of picturesque
romance, the work-a-day world is in danger
of appearing too dull and grey; after its
passions and heroisms and adventures the
common round is in danger of appearing stale and unprofitable. 'My life,' wrote
Flaubert when about eighteen years old,
'which I had dreamed was to be so full
of beauty and poetry and love, will be
like the rest, circumscribed, monotonous,
reasonable, stupid. I shall read for the law,
I shall get admitted; and then, for a fit
sequel, I shall go and live in some small
provincial town like Yvetot or Dieppe with
a post of *substitut* or *procureur du roi.*'

Emma Rouault's girlhood was nourished
on sentimental religion and romance. Her
first dream was of a life of ascetic ecstasy;
her next, a dream of a life of love and
passion. The actual life that destiny had in
store for her was a life to be dragged out by
the side of poor blundering Charles Bovary
in the blank monotony of Tostes and
Yonville l'Abbaye. Emma's sentiment was
false; how false, is pitilessly shown once

for all in the awed reverence she accords to
the senile and slobbering Duc de Laverdière
because he had been once the lover of a
queen. Yet there is pity in the breast of
the reader, more pity, as Sainte-Beuve
observes, than is in the breast of the author,
for the beautiful sentimental girl set in this
prison of stupidity and humdrum. Her life
is the tragedy of disillusion, from unhappy
marriage to unhappier sin, from sin to
suicide. In spite of disillusion Emma is
Emma to the last. Her suicide is as much
a bit of sentimentality as her sin ; and under
the very shadow of the great final disillusion,
she presses her dying lips to the crucifix
with the most passionate kiss of her whole
life.

For a generation Romanticism had been
dreaming sentimental dreams of passion
set free from the prose of ordinary restraints.
The novel of *Madame Bovary* was the
cruel, inevitable awakening. Flaubert's
irony was the appointed scourge for the
immoral sentimentality of French romance.
This is the justification, if justification there
can be, for a nakedness in certain scenes

which is abhorrent to English taste, abhorrent to all true taste. It is not only, as even
in his rebuke Sainte-Beuve admits, that the
picture of vice is not alluring, that the author
neither sympathises nor condones. The true
plea is that the stripping of romance from
vice is an essential part of the artistic motive.
Circe's swine must contemplate in the unflat-
tering mirror of truth the naked deformity
of their swinishness. Thus only were the
bewitched to be disenchanted.   It was one
of the humours of the Second Empire to
greet *Madame Bovary* with a criminal prose-
cution. It was whimsical, and yet a course
not difficult to understand, to spare Circe
and to punish Ulysses.

Emma Bovary entered upon life with all
the illusions of romance. She visited the
bitterness of her disillusion on the head of her
doting husband, who anticipated Mr. Casaubon's trick of making a noise over his soup.

Flaubert, who had entered upon life in
the glow of Romanticism, visited his disenchantment upon the provincial life about
him. With a touch of pathetic comedy
he has told us, in his preface to his friend

Bouilhet's *Dernières Chansons*, of the dreams
of himself and his companions in their
college days ; of their superb extravagance,
the last waves of Romanticism reaching
them in the provinces, and making the more
violent commotion in their brains, because
hemmed in by the barriers of provincial
conventionality. They used to be medieval
insurrectionary, Oriental ; carried daggers in
their pockets and so forth. Foolish enough
no doubt, and in no wise laudable, Flaubert
admits, but what hatred of commonplace !
what reverence for genius ! how we admired
Victor Hugo ! From sheer disgust with the
contrast of plain existence, one of his companions, he tells us, blew his brains out,
another hanged himself in his neckerchief.
Flaubert took another way ; he wrote
Madame Bovary. He avenged himself at
one blow on hated commonplace and betray-
ing Romanticism.

His aim, however, was neither to satirise
nor to moralise. Dissection, even, was in
his judgment a form of vengeance, and he
conceived that he had no call nor claim to
be a minister of vengeance. His aim was

simply to present the truth, to get to the soul of things, to reach and abide by what is essential in life. Of set purpose he turned his back on the accidental and dramatic. *Pas de monstres*, he exclaims, *et pas de héros*. No monsters and no heroes—that is a far cry from 1830 and Victor Hugo. Looked at closer it is not so far as it at first appears. It is really the next step, the step of reaction. After a certain amount of them, the mind fails to take seriously the theatricality of monsters and heroes. Then for a season the only reality that can pass itself off for real is the normal, the average, the unheroic. Flaubert's aim was simply to present life as it is. He succeeded to a miracle in presenting life as he saw it with eyes from which had just dropped the coloured glasses of Romanticism. Life, unhappily, is only too full of monsters and monstrosities ; the boon of a free Press does not allow us to forget them for a moment. Life has, too, Heaven be praised for it, its heroisms beyond the skill of romance to surpass, its heroes from Gordon to Alice Ayres. No monsters and no heroes,—that is not reality.

It is but the reality visible in the reaction from romance. It is the art of disillusion.

But with Flaubert it is art. That is the important point for literary criticism. It is not 'naturalism.' It is not the complacent copying of commonplace; nor is it a scraping with a muck-rake for the muck's sake We know from Guy de Maupassant, who served a literary apprenticeship with him, that Flaubert, in spite of his great friendship for M. Zola and his great admiration for his vigorous talent, never forgave him his naturalism. Flaubert, caustically remarks his talented disciple, was no mere Realist because he observed life with care any more then M. Cherbuliez is an Idealist because he observes life badly. Art, ideal as it necessarily is, cannot do without observation, but its kingdom cometh not with observation alone. It penetrates to the spirit and reveals the significance of the things observed. *Madame Bovary* is art by its intensity of vision, by its inevitableness, by its style. It is a vision of a certain order of life, penetrating, essential and complete, told in incomparable language. So unerring, so convincing is the truth of the vision, so entirely is it without the ornament, the surprises, the bending and trimming of fact, which had been customary in romance, that it is little wonder that the cry has been raised, whether for praise or blame,—'This is not art; this is life itself.' The cry is intelligible, but it is a very ambiguous piece of praise. In *Anna Karénine* there is an episode, which, according to Matthew Arnold, turns out to import absolutely nothing, and to be introduced solely to give the author the pleasure of telling us that all Levine's shirts had been packed up. 'Look,' said Arnold in effect. 'It leads to nothing. That is how things happen in life. This is not art; this is a piece of life itself.' No, it is not a piece of life itself. It is only rather poor art. It falls between the two stools of reality and real art. Between life and a book there must always remain a great gulf fixed. To merely copy in art the apparently meaningless, anomalous, or unintelligible things of life, on the plea that such things do actually exist, is to mistake the whole aim and scope

of art. Many able writers, no doubt, in
order to cheat the reader into taking their
story for matter of fact, have employed
the device of putting in bits of unnecessary
information. It is a trick as old as Defoe.
Flaubert's method is the exact contrary.
He is real by piercing to the essence of
things, by selecting the necessary and inevitable in life. No ordinary life to ordinary
eyes was ever so natural as Emma Bovary's,
so free from surprises and accidents. It is
life, but life pictured in the seer's vision of
fate. The dulness and humdrum of life are
so seized by art that they are no longer dull
and humdrum, but have become poignant
tragedy, searching our hearts with pity and
terror. And with all its accuracy of observation, and all its science, the leaven of
Romanticism is present and active. Thence
that wonderful prose fashioned by Flaubert
with incredible effort out of the resources
bequeathed by Chateaubriand and Gautier,
with its sound, its colour, its fastidious use
of an abounding vocabulary. Thence the
vivid beauty of the pictures which detach
themselves from the narrative and have the

distinction and distinctness of fine painting.
Thence the perpetual beating as of an unre-
solved discord between experience and
aspiration, every dissonance in the inevitable
progression of suspended discords gaining
its poignancy from its suggestion of the full
romantic chord.

Sainte-Beuve quarrels with this persistent
poignancy of dissonance as at once a flaw in
art, and a failure in truth.   That it is not the
whole truth has already been insisted on.
No doubt even Tostes and Yonville l'Abbaye
might have yielded something better than
the uniform unloveliness of Emma's surroundings, some beautiful soul, some charm
of first love or glory of self-sacrifice.   George
Sand, who with consistently Rousseau-like
sentiment had passed from singing the woes
of the *femme incomprise* to painting village
idylls, was likewise offended by the unvary-
ing bitterness of Flaubert's tone, and urged
him to turn his unrivalled vision in a similar
direction.   Flaubert admired George Sand's
work heartily, unaffectedly, without reserva-
tion.   But these idylls he must leave to her.
She charmed, but she did not convince.   He

must convince, and he felt that he could never convince with the rose-coloured village idyll. He was a critical master of method. He divined that happy accident, convenient coincidence, consoling conversion of character, all the things which go to make up the very essence of the charm of romance, are out of place in that novel of ordinary life, which as the fundamental element of its artistic effect seeks first of all to convince. From his standpoint and for his purposes, they were part of that accidental and dramatic on which he must resolutely turn his back. It was not enough that his incident might have happened, he must tie himself down to the things that must have happened. Balzac has somewhere a saying to the effect that the actual happening of unlikely things is the only excuse for their unlikelihood; and that accordingly in fiction, where there can be no actual happening, unlikely things are without excuse. This is a saying that has no application to romance. Romance convinces by pleasing; in it the wildest improbability justifies itself by beauty and imaginative propriety. But *Madame Bovary* must please by convincing. Of the axiom of art contained in Balzac's saying *Madame Bovary* is a more perfect illustration than any story of Balzac's own, more perfect even than *Eugénie Grandet.*

Flaubert, too, coming quite at the end of the stir of Romanticism, was addressing an audience which had been glutted with the romantic. Beauty, strength, prowess, heroism, striking incident and intricate situation had all come to be regarded as so much stock-property of romance ; and, to a taste grown critical and scientific after a surfeit of romance, were tainted with something of romantic unreality. Art less inexorable than *Madame Bovary* would have been in danger of appearing sentimental, or merely pretty or picturesque. So Flaubert denied himself things beautiful and engaging in themselves. The solitary exception is the physical beauty of Emma ; and this exception is as significant as the rule. In romance the beauty of woman is a spell and a power. It dominates, bewitches, maddens, consoles, inspires, glorifies. It is a counterpoise to the power of princes, stronger than the policy of states-

men. Kings yield to it, heroes live and die
for it. That is the kind of sway Emma
would love to dream of; and her beauty
served but to procure for her two heartless
and vulgar intrigues with a soulless libertine
and a pusillanimous sentimentalist. Through
all her life the shadow of sordid evil is on
her beauty; and after the dreadful death, we
are forced to sit beside the corpse through
the watches of the night, to mark that this
beauty, too, was an illusion that must pass,
and with shrinking eyes to observe it under
the befouling touch of dissolution.

So again in the matter of incident. After
the intoxicating wealth of incident in romance, Flaubert is temperate to the verge of
total abstinence. In romance the seemingly
most trivial occurrence leads infallibly,
through devious and delightful ways, to
death or victory. A face seen by chance in
a crowd is certain to reappear in the crisis of
your fate. One glance from a pair of bright
eyes, and you find yourself entangled hand
and foot in inextricable and far-reaching
threads of crime or conspiracy. A hasty
word to a stranger in a tavern, and your

humble destiny is interwoven with the plots
and passions of queen and cardinal. Wan-
derings about strange streets and into unknown houses always lead to something
fateful—a glimpse of a girl to be followed
and sought thenceforward amid danger and
intrigue through mazes of entrancing mystery, or the awakening of some malignant
enmity never thereafter to cease to haunt
your path. And the infinite delight of it all !
Only unfortunately things do not happen so
at Tostes or Yonville l'Abbaye ; or if they
did, the critical reader would want for it
something better than the bare word of the
novelist. When Emma goes to the ball at
the Château, the scent of the old romance-
reader sniffs a plot at last. When she enters
with alacrity upon her first flirtation, his nose
is down on the trail,—to come to a prompt
check, however. The aristocratic admirer of
the night before rides by as she is on her way
homeward ; and they never meet again.
That is not how meetings end in romance.
Yet in this meeting there was a fatefulness
so awful in its implacable necessity, that
beside it the fate of romance is but a play-

ing at fate. The man who flirted with her perhaps never gave her another thought; perhaps recollected his passing attentions as a meritorious act of good-nature to the pretty woman who seemed to know no one of all the company. And he had given a human soul the little determining push over the edge of the inclined plane, down which it must slide through sin and degradation to the self-inflicted death by poison. So it is with the rest of what we must call the incidents of the novel, such as the removal to Yonville, or the first platonic philandering with Léon. This is the only species of incident that Flaubert allows himself. Striking incident or co-incidence would savour of the accidental, would awake suspicion of arrangement, of artifice. His incidents must be necessary and inevitable. They can therefore have no decorative or romantic beauty; their interest is purely tragic; they are but moments in the unfolding of fate in the soul of Emma Bovary.

It is assuredly a sombre and pitiless story; but the truth was, that for Flaubert's epoch the satisfying charm of the simpler cadences had been lost by over-much familiarity. No

idyllic prettiness of presentation could bring
before the mind with the force of Flaubert's
irony the romance and passion possible to
the dullest human life. Upon her return
from the famous ball, the stamp of middle
class which was on her husband and her
home, the total lack of the style for which
she yearned, were to Emma irritating,
intolerable, nauseating. And by her side
her fond, awkward husband is rubbing his
hands with satisfaction at finding himself at
home again. Or again later, when Emma
has fallen lower, Bovary, returning in the
middle of the night from a visit to a patient,
is afraid to awake his wife. By the flickering
light of the china night-lamp he sees dimly
the closed white curtains of his little
daughter's cot by the bed-side. He thinks
he hears her light breathing, and straightway
falls to making plans for her future. He
sees the little thing gradually growing up
into a girl, into a woman. He will save
money and take a little farm in the country.
How happy they will be, they three together! When she is fifteen she will be
beautiful like her mother, and will wear large

straw hats in the summer, so that the two
will look like sisters in the distance. And
then some good fellow will be found to
marry her; he will make her happy; it will
go on like that always. But Emma is not
really asleep; she, too, is dreaming her
dream. She has fled with her lover to some
strange, new country whence they will never
return. They wander and wander silent, en-
twined in each other's arms. From mountain
tops they catch glimpses of foreign-looking
towns, with domes, and bridges, and ships,
and forests of citron trees, and cathedrals of
white marble; or they stand amidst the
mingled sounds of bells, and the neighing of
mules, and the murmur of guitars, and the
splash of fountains, with statues gleaming
under their veil of water, the spray sprink-
ling the fruit piled at their feet; or they are
entering a fishing-village in the evening,
where the brown nets are drying in the wind
along the cliff in front of the huts—somewhere away from this home and this husband,
in the picturesque realms of romance. And
romance, which would have been no dream,
lay at her feet in poor Yonville l'Abbaye;

only, blinded and perverted by the false
romantic, she passed it by, and could not see
it. With motherhood might have come the
real bliss and glory, which only begin where
the romance of art leaves off. The village
idyll is no fiction of literature. Nay, the
climax of the husband's blundering incapacity, the day of his deepest humiliation,
might have been the wife's supreme triumph.
There was amongst the Bovarys' acquaintance in Yonville l'Abbaye a man named
Homais, an apothecary, a typical specimen
of the provincial scientific smatterer. He
gets his opinions and his knowledge ready-
made from Parisian journals; and finds a
vent for his self-importance in writing letters
to the local prints. He reads in a medical
paper of a new surgical operation for club-
feet. There was a stable-boy at the village
inn with a club-foot, and forthwith he scents
a promising scheme of self-advertisement.
He writes paragraphs to air his knowledge,
hinting that Yonville l'Abbaye is not so far
behind Paris in matters scientific and surgical as it is the fashion to suppose. He
understands that their clever townsman,

M. Bovary, is likely to undertake this famous
operation. Unhappy doctor! unhappy
cripple! they shrink both equally from the
experiment. The boy, having been club-
footed from birth, was accustomed to his lot,
and dreaded the pain and danger; Bovary
knew in his heart that he was but a bungler
in far less critical operations. Both victims
flutter against their fate in vain. The boy is
taunted with cowardice, cajoled with flattering promises of straight limbs and maidens'
smiles. Bovary, sick at heart with nervous
dread, is urged forward by Homais and the
talk Homais has evoked. But it is his wife
who binds him to the stake. Her romantic
sentiment is aroused ; if her husband were to
become a celebrity, she might almost like
him. The operation is performed. After a
deceitful appearance of success followed by a
sickening interval of suspense, mortification
sets in. Another surgeon has to be sent for,
and the limb has to be amputated. Bovary
dares not cross the threshold of his house ;
he cowers inside, his head on his breast, his
hands clasped, his eyes fixed ; the screams
of the boy reach him from across the narrow

street. In his misery he turns to his wife for comfort, and she repulses him with passionate contempt. The pain of it all is almost more than we can bear. But with what force the dissonance suggests the harmony of a true home and true wifehood! the world outside indignant, contemptuous, cruel ; inside, husband and wife and love. If, after her struggles and temptation and sins, Emma had had that grace of womanhood and wifehood left in her to be stirred by this bitter suffering, even then the seven devils had come out of her. Love had turned the mean surroundings, the stupidity, the suffering, to ' a blaze of joy and a crash of song.'

The episode of the club-foot has been put in the fore-front of their objections by friends and foes. It has been criticised as a piece of naturalism, as mere ugliness, as but an occasion to indulge in description of painful and unnecessary detail. Flaubert's method of setting everything before the reader as distinct and vivid as language will make it is, of course, open to serious criticism, when he has to treat of things which are physically or morally revolting. Whether in this

episode the artist has wrung music out of the
dissonance, whether out of the strong he has
succeeded in bringing forth a strange, new,
bitter sweet—that is a question upon which
taste may be expected always to differ. But
it is not naturalism, it is not mere ugliness.
It is an integral part of the spiritual tragedy,
the fatal triumph of half science and false
sentiment; it is the revealing instance to
exhibit Emma's heart, that was a living heart
once, morally paralysed by indulged sentimentality. And it is a turning-point in the
action. It is this last revelation of her husband's uninteresting incapacity which urges
her tottering soul to its final plunge to
perdition.

'Moralist, you know everything, but you
are cruel.' It is in these words that Sainte-
Beuve apostrophises the creator of *Madame
Bovary*. Cruelty there is in his unrelenting
irony, cruelty born of the bitterness of disillusion towards the commonplace, but
cruelty chiefly towards sentimentality and
ignorant self-conceit. And knowledge there
is, deep, wide, minute. And a moral there is,
as there must always be in any true picture

of life ; a moral, guiltless as Flaubert is of
seeking to enforce a moral, almost painful in
its force.   But first and last, there is art :
art in the intensity of vision that pierces
beneath the surface of fact ; art in the note
of tragedy, the inevitable march of fate ; art
in the scrupulous avoidance of everything
not essential to the idea ; art in the imper-
sonal directness of presentation ; art in the
style.

ROMANCE AND YOUTH

A YEAR or two ago M. Ferdinand Brunetière, the austere literary critic of the *Revue
des Deux Mondes*, delivered a lecture at the
Odéon Theatre upon Molière's *L'Ecole des
Femmes*. According to him, so M. Lemaître
reported, the comedy turned upon the
question of age. Agnes is sixteen; Arnolphe confesses to forty-two. That in itself is
enough in the play to make Arnolphe not
only ridiculous but odious from beginning
to end. His successful rival Horace is
twenty. He has nothing but youth to
recommend him; nor is anything more
needed. He and Agnes have all the
sympathy of author and audience. And
quite right too! cries this austere M. Brunetière; it is a natural and sacred law. In
sympathising with Agnes and Horace, the

heart is sympathising with nature and instinct.

Molière perhaps does not make the play turn quite so nakedly on the contrast of age as the moral requires. There may not be much in Horace's favour beside his youth; but there is a good deal more than his forty-two years to be set to the discredit of Arnolphe. He is a system-monger and an egotist. Now the egotist, according to Mr. Meredith, is the chosen sport of the comic spirit; while woman (bless her!) was created to be the bane of system and the despair of the system-monger. When a mature bachelor like Arnolphe, in self-conscious dread of becoming as one of the horned herd of husbands about him, captures a babe in long clothes and has her mewed up and artificially trained to be a helpmeet for his special lordship, then the imps of mischief gather in a circle on their haunches to wait and watch for the catastrophe. And if the wretched man, after dwarfing the girl's nature and bounding her horizon, demands love on the score of gratitude, the angels of heaven join in the applause over his discomfiture.

Arnolphe's whole conduct was unfair and ignoble, and the heart of the natural man rejoices to see his prey escape him.

Still, whether or not the comedy was exclusively framed to point this moral, the moral is unquestionably there. Arnolphe's forty-two years count heavily against him. Literature in the mouths of the dramatist and the critic is definitely enough on the side of youth against middle age. Nor could spokesmen be selected for literature less open to suspicion of sentimental bias. As a critic M. Brunetière has been reproached with being too much of a schoolmaster and too little of a lover. And as for Molière, he is the incarnation of that spirit of comedy which is the arch foe of sentimentalism.

So much for the doctrine of literature; now for the teaching of life. Shift the scene from the French stage to the Bow Street Police-Court. A defendant, aged twenty-one, described as a pianoforte-tuner, is charged with being drunk and disorderly and with assaulting the police. The police, it appeared, had interfered to protect a

woman, whom prisoner was threatening.
Magistrate. — 'Who was the woman?'
Prisoner.—' My wife, your worship.' *Magistrate.*—' Your wife! why you have the
appearance of a boy. Is your wife here?'
She was. A little woman stepped forward
and said she was prisoner's wife. She was
nineteen. They had been married twelve
months. Then the scandalised magistrate
delivered his soul. 'There is no place,' he
exclaimed, 'where so much misery is seen
as at the police-court. There is no place to
see so plainly how human misery is produced
by human folly,—not by bad laws but by
human folly. A boy and girl, just beyond
the age when they ought to be whipped, go
and get married!'

The age when they ought to be whipped!
Shades of Romeo and Juliet! You see,
instead of applauding a natural and sacred
law M. Brunctière ought to have laid
Horace and Agnes across his knee, and
imagined for a moment he held under his
admonitory palm the prostrate form of M.
Zola. It is painful to think what would
have been the worthy magistrate's feelings

could the precocious babes of Verona have
been dragged before his judgment-seat,
Indeed if Romeo and Juliet could be translated with their ages unchanged from the
poetry of Shakespeare into the prose of
modern London life, the stringency of our
legislation would make it awkward for the
lover of a lady of such tender years.
Happily those immortal types of youth
and romance, of passionate and tragic love,
were not within the jurisdiction. They were
Italian, Italians of the Renaissance; and
Italians have a large licence in these matters.
It is the naughty sun, as Byron explains,
and the naughtier moon. Sun and race
make a deal of difference. Do you remember the Indian girl in Mr. Kipling's beautiful
story, 'Without Benefit of Clergy,' and her
rebellious jealousy of the protracted youth
of the 'white *mem-log*,' her rivals?

Perhaps the sun of Italy is indirectly
answerable for the tender age of the lovers
and their lasses in much of English poetry
and romance. Our poets and romancers
were so long under the influence of Italy
and the Renaissance. From the time that

Chaucer transferred his allegiance from
French to Italian models, until the prestige of the *grand siècle* and Charles II.'s
connection with the court of Louis XIV.
reimposed a French model, Italy set our
literary fashion. The tragedy of Webster
and the like but reflects the Italy of the
Sforzas and Borgias. Boccaccio and Ban-
dello were our models for story-telling.
With the form of the sonnet we imported
from Italy the spirit and features of Italian
sonneteering. Italian Juliets were imported
into English poetry and romance without
being made to pay the duty of added years
to a northern climate. What in Italy had
been nature became in England a piece of
literary convention. The Elizabethan son-
neteer, if he was not chanting the mature
divinity of the Virgin Queen, would proclaim
his devotion to some lady-love of traditional
immaturity. At Juliet's age, the English
miss is apt, as Byron brutally said, to smell
of bread and butter. No sober Briton
nowadays toasts the maiden of blushing
fifteen,—at least not within earshot of the
police. Charles Surface and his friends were

not a particularly sober crew; but in these days Joseph Surface would belong to a Vigilance Society and there might be the devil to pay. It is absolutely incomprehensible how Robert Browning, of all men in the world, should have come to make Mildred Tresham only fourteen years of age when she brought the blot on the 'scutcheon. Dr. Furnivall really should have seen to this. Evelyn Hope was sixteen years old when she died, and the man of forty-eight who loved her confessed that it was not 'her time to love,' and that only somewhere in the seventh heaven could he look for any return.

It is true that to redress the balance romance has some mature heroines to set in the opposite scale. To begin with, there is Helen of Troy herself, the arch-heroine of romance. Her love affairs began early enough no doubt, early enough to satisfy Mr. Browning. She was a mere child when Theseus ran away with her. But by a shameless statistical inquiry, by reckoning up the episodes of her youth, and by comparing the date of the Argonautic expedition,

in which her brothers took part, with the date
of the Trojan war, the unconscionable Bayle
proved to his own ungentlemanly satisfaction
that Helen was fifty, more or less, when Paris
carried her off in triumph to Troy. Well,
then the war lasted ten years; and at the
end of it, not only was Menelaus legitimately
proud to get her back again, but her beauty
was so potent still that Priam forgot and
forgave in his pride of it all the woes it had
brought on him and his, and paid his tribute
of kingly courtesy to her unabdicated grace
of womanhood. Nay, ten years later again,
when Telemachus visited the Spartan court
in quest of news of his many-wiled and
much-wanted father, Helen was a fine
woman still, though at that time, by Bayle's
iniquitous calculations, no less than seventy
years of age. No doubt her race and
lineage must be borne in mind. There is
an elderly aristocratic couple in one of
Disraeli's novels, or in one of the parodies of
his novels—it is difficult sometimes to remember with Disraeli which is text and
which is parody—who might have been
taken, so pure was their blood and so perfect

their breeding, for their eldest son and daughter's eldest son and daughter. Helen's lineage was more than aristocratic; it was divine. Daughter of Zeus and Leda, sister of Castor and Pollux, she had in her veins the eternal ichor of the gods. That of course made a difference. Indeed Bayle takes credit for the moderation of his estimate, and hints that some would make her out to be at least a hundred. But I linger too long over the ungallant gossip of this dictionary-making sceptic. It was unworthy of a Frenchman to canvass the age of the liege-lady of all lovers of romance. It was unworthy of the caution of a scientific sceptic to clutch at the conjectural chronology of mythological fancy.

If you listen to some of the gossips by the way, you would believe that Iphigenia was not Agamemnon's daughter, but the daughter of Helen and Theseus. That would make Helen under thirty (would it not?) when she eloped with Paris. It adds fresh cruelty to the curse that blasted Iphigenia's youth, to think that it was her own mother that was the cause. But she would not be the last daughter who has been sacrificed to a mother's flirtation.

If Helen had a grown-up daughter when her face was the fate of nations, Penelope had a grown-up son when the stress of rivalry for her hand was at its keenest. The suitors very likely had set their hearts at least as much upon the estate as on the person of this paragon of prehistoric grass-widowhood. That is what cynicism would suggest, and there was not a little in the conduct of the suitors to give colour to the suggestion. Yet Homer hardly gives us to understand that Penelope was past the prime of her beauty. Nor did scandal spare even her name. The good Homer gave no countenance to it, or it would have put a very distressing complexion on the pretty story of the woven and unwoven web. One version of the birth of Pan, remember, was that he was born of Penelope in her lord's absence, and that no single suitor could claim the whole credit of the paternity. Pan, you know, had horns and hoofs.

Pass from romance of legend to romance of history. The wedded names of Antony and Cleopatra remain hardly less than Tristram and Iseult the very symbol of

love's lordship. Now Cleopatra was twenty-
one when first she met 'broad-fronted Cæsar,'
and was twenty-five before the thoughtful
knife of Brutus cut the *liaison* short. Yet
these were the green and salad days whereof
Shakespeare makes her speak so scornfully.
When she captivated Mark Antony she was
twenty-eight, and she held him her slave for
eleven whole years ; so that when 'by the
aspick's bite' she 'died a queen,' absolute
queen of him still soul and sense, she was of
the unromantic age of thirty-nine. I named
Iseult. A learned friend of mine has un-
earthed her epitaph from an old Italian book,
whereby it appears she was thirty-one at
the time when she fell stricken to death on
Tristram's corpse.

So, you see, it was no such revolutionary
innovation, no such Copernican discovery
for romance, when Balzac made his much
vaunted 'woman of thirty' the centre of the
system of his human comedy. The usually
unsympathetic Sainte-Beuve might trumpet
the achievement, and talk of these women
of thirty waiting dumb and expectant for
their discoverer, and of the electric flash

when they met. But really she is an old
friend in romance, this woman of thirty!
Nor did Charles de Bernard do any new
thing when he bettered his master and gave
the world his 'woman of forty.' Nor did
Thackeray, when, by one of the boldest
strokes in fiction, he made Harry Esmond
turn from Beatrix to her mother Lady
Castlewood. Diane de Poitiers was forty-
eight when Henry II. of France was twenty-
nine. The young King surrendered at
discretion to his enchantress, and gave her
his country, himself, ay and his queen too,
to do what she would with. She held her
sway without check or wane to the end.
She was seventy when Brantôme saw her,
and she was, he says, as fair and fresh and
lovable as at thirty. Posterity, said Paul
de St. Victor prettily, still looks at Diane
through the dazzled eyes of Henry; and
we picture her always, in spite of her really
venerable age, as the artists of the Renaissance immortalised her, in the form of Jean
Goujon's goddesses or Cellini's nymph.

Then there is the famous case of Ninon
de l'Enclos. If Ninon was only thirty when

she carried off captive Madame de Sévigné's husband, she was full fifty-five when a generation later she took captive the same Madame de Sévigné's son. And so far as the willingness of the spirit went, she would no doubt have carried her conquests into the third generation, but that the Marquis de Grignan, Madame de Sévigné's grandson, was barely fifteen when she was seventy— the three-score years and ten assigned by the preacher as the limits of life, not of love. Like Emma Bovary, Ninon kept her last kiss for the cross ; she devoted to religion the last two or three of the eighty-nine years allotted to her as the span of her earthly pilgrimage.

I have been led far afield by my dream of fair women—even the census-taker has his dreams, though it is his invidious duty to ask the ladies' ages. I was thinking rather of the heroes than of the heroines of romance when I started with the contrast between the views of the police-magistrate and the literary critic. As to the age of romance for girls there is no great discrepancy between the ideas expressed in

literature and those entertained in life. Our
Psyches are still girls, if our Cupids begin
to wax fat and forty. Neither the tragic
childhood of Mildred Tresham nor the triumphant old age of Ninon de l'Enclos is normal
in life or books. Nor, in spite of Sainte-
Beuve and the enthusiasm of later and lesser
critics, is Balzac's woman of thirty a normal
subject of romance. She was bred partly
of Balzac's idiosyncrasy, partly of his pride
of originality, partly of artificial social conditions. The Baby's Grandmother in Mrs.
Walford's amusing novel was not regarded
by her neighbours as a normal case, least of
all by the baby's very conventional parents.
It is significant, as M. Lemaître has observed, that Molière's Agnes is still made up
on the modern stage to look sixteen or
thereabouts; whereas the actor who plays
Arnolphe to produce the proper effect is
bound to add, and in fact always does add,
a very considerable number of years to the
forty-two Molière gave him. To a modern
audience a prospective husband of forty-two
would appear at least as natural as a prospective husband of twenty. And if in life

the man of forty-two is not such a terror to
the girls as he was in the old comedy, so
neither is the youth of twenty such a hero.
What strikes one in the old-fashioned stories
is the extraordinary capacities of the hero
of twenty. There is hardly anything he
cannot do. In peace and war, in policy and
passion, he is equal to all emergencies. In
reality the youth of twenty is not of much
account. The girls snub him; his college
gates him; nobody but his tailor trusts him
much. The pianoforte-tuner was twenty-one;
and a gentleman with judicial experience
of life and humanity regards him as a boy
just beyond the age when he ought to be
whipped. The young Duke of Orleans was
of the full heroic age of twenty-one when he
sought to take his place in the ranks and
was put in prison for his pains; and whether
for sympathy or sarcasm the world was
agreed in treating his exploit as the prank
of a school-boy. At the Bar men are still
rising juniors with grey hair or bald head.
In politics Mr. Chamberlain is a young man
Mr. Balfour is almost a boy, Mr. Curzon is
positively an infant, though no doubt a pre-

cocious infant. Used men to ripen earlier'
or was the world's work simpler? Or has
romance been at her tricks, and have we
here another of those grievous discrepancies
between fact and old-fashioned fiction which
make Mr. Howells to go so heavily?

Old Montaigne did actually fix the age of
full maturity at twenty. Like Lord Beacons-
field, he was a believer in youth. Even at
his epoch he thought men ought to set about
the world's work earlier than they did. ' For
my part' (I quote the quaint phrases of John
Florio's translation which Shakespeare used)
' I think that our minds are as full grown and
perfectly jointed at twenty years as they
shall be, and promise as much as they can. A
mind which at that age hath not given some
evident token or earnest of her sufficiency,
shall hardly give it afterward, put her to what
trial you list. Natural qualities and virtues,
if they have any vigorous or beauteous thing
in them, will produce and show the same
within that time or never.' Yet even with
him twenty is the age rather of promise than
performance, and when the talk is of actions
he raises his limit to thirty. ' Of all humane,

honourable, and glorious actions that ever
came into my knowledge, I am persuaded I
should have a harder task to number those
which both in ancient times and in our own
have been produced and achieved before the
age of thirty years than such as were performed after. Yea, often in the life of the
same men.' Yet the only cases he cites are
Hannibal, and his 'great adversary,' Scipio.
'Both lived,' says Montaigne, 'the better part
of their life with the glory which they had
gotten in their youth ; and though afterward
they were great men in respect of all others,
yet were they but mean in regard of themselves.' *Ultima primis cedebant* was Livy's
sentence on Scipio. Hannibal was twenty-
nine when he invaded Italy. Scipio was
thirty-two at Zama, but that was only the
crowning victory of his second or third cam-
paign ; he had saved his father's life in a
battle at the age of sixteen, and at eighteen
he fought on the fatal field of Cannæ.

Bacon, who was inclined to agree with
Montaigne as to the advantage of youth,
does not add many instances. He quotes
Cosimo who was appointed Duke of Florence

in 1573 at the age of seventeen and proved
an able ruler ; also a certain Gaston de Foix.
According to Bacon's last editor, this was
probably a Viscount de Béarn, born in 1331,
who served with distinction at the age of
fourteen in military and then in civil business
and was described in his later years by
Froissart as a pattern of chivalry. Cosimo
governed a wily and turbulent population at
seventeen, and Augustus Cæsar by his brain
and by his arm was master of the world at
nineteen. Montaigne thought it an anomaly
that the same Augustus, 'that had been universal and supreme judge of the world when
he was but nineteen years old, would by his
laws have another to be thirty before he
should be made a competent judge of a
cottage or farm.' But Augustus Cæsar was
an exceptionally wise youth. And yet,—
perhaps because, as Lady Blandish hinted,
Love does not love exceptionally wise youths,
—Cleopatra, who was an expert in love,
would have none of him as a lover. Our own
Pitt, who, as we are so often reminded, was a
minister at twenty-three, as a lover cut no
figure at all.

How came Montaigne and Bacon to leave out Alexander? Early in his twenties he had added the conquest of Asia to the conquest of Greece. Before he died at thirty-two he had married three wives, and sighed for more worlds to conquer; and besides his unparalleled achievement, he was as beautiful as a god, if the sculptors are to be trusted. He might perhaps have put his youth to better purpose than to running after Thais and setting fire to Persepolis, but his marriage with the fair Roxana, the captive of his bow and spear, was after the most orthodox romantic pattern. Then there was the great Condé. He was, I believe, ill-favoured, though I have a portrait which makes him fine-looking. But any way was not the conqueror of Rocroi at twenty-two a hero to fire a girl's imagination? And any woman, in romance or out of it, might have been proud to have had for lover the famous Duc de La Rochefoucauld, with his youth, his handsome face, his clever tongue, and his reckless bravery. Indeed, as a matter of history, a gracious line of remarkable women were proud to have him for their lover.

But these men were exceptions. They only prove the rule. And if I ransacked history for more instances they would be exceptions still. The normal youth of twenty is not at all the omnipotent person that the fancy of romance has painted him. Accordingly, when the novelists took to copying life instead of correcting it, they came round to the magistrate's way of thinking, and the age of the hero went up. I imagine that the hero of twenty is an exception in the ordinary modern novel of ordinary life. Poor Pendennis at twenty was very little of a hero. He may fall in love with a Fotheringay, but a Fotheringay will hardly be so weak as to fall in love with him. If a Laura love him, she will wait and watch for him to grow into a man. Miss Ethel Newcome will flirt with Clive with a light heart, but could she be expected to think of the boy seriously? Jane Austen's Emma, who thoroughly knew her way about in matchmaking, surrendered her heart to the safe keeping of thirty-eight—such was the sober age of the admirable Knightley. Jane Eyre's Rochester was certainly no chicken. If you were to apply the brutal methods of Bayle to Ouida's Tricotrin, I believe (though I have never worked it out myself, being a poor hand at figures) that it would turn out that Tricotrin had attained the respectable age of seventy or eighty, when he cheats us of our tears by his apparently premature death at the barricades. Miss Broughton's magnificent ugly men are eminently mature. They are scarred and seamed with experiences like Milton's Satan. And (to the no small surprise of some of the clever novelist's sincerest admirers) Miss Broughton has been ranked high among English realists by no less a critic than M. Brunetière, and held up as a pattern to certain of his own countrymen who make a great cry of their realism—and no little wool.

Ah, Molière might say, this may be life, but it is not nature. M. Brunetière reiterates his point. He argues in his new volume of *Critical Essays on the History of French Literature* that Molière's moral was always for a return to nature from unnatural convention ; from conventional and unnatural marriage, social fashions, morality, religion.

Well, what precisely is meant by nature?
There is an obvious truth and a number of
unobvious fallacies in the ordinary distinction
between nature and civilisation. A philosopher, whom M. Brunetière knows a great
deal better than I do, taught long ago once
for all that it is man's nature to be civilised ;
and the sentiments and usages of civilisation
—as I think M. Lemaître has urged in
answer to M. Brunetière—mould and control
even the instinctive impulses of love and
passion. Where in history would Molière
find his golden age or state of nature wherein
the girls of sixteen fall in love only with the
boys of twenty? Nausicaa's girl's-heart was
given almost at first sight to the middle-aged
and much enduring hero, who had a wife and
grown-up son and several other things await-
ing him at home. It is one of the oldest and
prettiest love stories in the world. And if
you think that Ulysses got some unfair
advantage from the grace that Athena shed
about his head and shoulders, when, the
maidens looking the other way, he made
his toilet on the sea-shore, what do you say
to the case of Desdemona and her Moor?

And if Shakespeare's word is not evidence, what do you say of Vanessa and Swift? A girl's instinct, according to Mr. Meredith, who is notoriously in the secrets of the sex, is for strength. This is, no doubt, a survival from the old-fashioned days when women used to look to men as their protectors and defenders. Well, strength is displayed in different ways in different ages and societies. So far as feats of chivalry went and Homeric derring-do, there was no particular reason, perhaps, why a youth should not be a hero so soon as his muscle was set. It has sometimes struck me in reading the *Iliad*, that the Trojan War was liker to modern games than to modern warfare. On the half-holidays, so to speak, when the weather was fine, the Greeks and Trojans would turn out for a match on the ringing plains, while the old boys looked on from the walls and the ships. Our playgrounds and hunting-fields could show almost as good a record of damage to life and limb as was suffered by the heroes in many an Homeric combat or medieval tourney. But if the girl's instinct is for a man strong in her particular sphere—political, intellectual, or social; if her hero is to be a man among men in complex stages of society, she must put up with a lover of a certain age.

So much the worse for civilisation, Molière might insist, It is nature that speaks in the poetry and romance of the love of boy and girl. It is nature that speaks in the spectator's instinctive sympathy with the young lovers in the comedies. It is a natural and sacred law that youth should love youth. When civilisation puts youth and youth asunder, man is dividing what nature would join. And if history can produce no such golden age or state of nature an appeal might be made to the customs of the proletariat. The very name *proletariat* is warrant enough. Undistracted by conventional ambitions, and undeterred by conventional scruples, the proletariat increases and multiplies at an age which makes magistrates and Malthusians, economists and the guardians of the poor, tear their hair in dismay and indignation. And George Sand might be called to support the appeal. George Sand, of all women, could for opposite reasons have had no pre-

judices in favour of immaturity in marriage
or love. Yet when she turned to study the
country people about her at Nohant and to
pourtray it in those charming village tales
she wrote towards the close of her full-blooded
career, the popular sentiment therein is
definitely, not to say despotically, on M.
Brunetière's side. 'Germain,' says Maurice
to his son-in-law, in *La Mare au Diable*,
'you must make up your mind to take
another wife. It is two years since my
daughter died, and your eldest boy is seven.
You are going on for thirty, and after that
a man is too old to marry.' And then he
proceeds to recommend Germain not to
think of a young girl, but to look out for a
seasoned widow of his own years. Germain
in fact was only twenty-eight; but he regarded himself, and was generally regarded
by his neighbours, as too old to be the
husband of a young girl. So when he fell
in love with Marie, who was sixteen, he did
not dare tell her of his feelings; and when
he married her, it was something of a scandal
in the country-side.

Then Dickens, again. How Dickens loved

to watch the boys and girls falling in love
and marrying! Think of Tommy Traddles,
defiant of conventionality, triumphantly playing Puss in the Corner with his five sisters-in-
law in his business chambers at Gray's Inn;
or of Scrooge's nephew and Scrooge's niece
by marriage and Scrooge's niece's sisters at
the ghostly Christmas party, and the shameless way Topper followed up the plump
sister with the lace tucker at the game of
Blind Man's Buff. 'Why did you get
married?' Scrooge had asked his nephew
on the Christmas Eve in return for his
Christmas greetings. 'Because I fell in love.'
'Because you fell in love!' growled Scrooge,
as if that were the only thing in the world
more ridiculous than a merry Christmas.
Ebenezer Scrooge, you may remember,
boasted that he helped to support the institutions of civilisation, the prison and the
workhouse; and if the boys and girls must
marry, and then when want came would
rather die than take advantage of these
institutions,—well, they had better die, he
said, and decrease the surplus population. Or
take *Bleak House.* The Court of Chancery and

the great case of Jarndyce against Jarndyce
—there you have, no doubt, a triumph of
civilisation ; but Richard Carstone and Ada,
with their young love, had nature on their side.
Richard confessed upon his deathbed that
he had wedded his girl-wife to want, and
that he had the world still to begin. Yet
they had their reward.

Let us consult one more authority. Sir
Austin Absworthy Bearne Feverel, Baronet,
of Raynham Abbey, had, like our worthy
magistrate, meditated deeply upon life and
marriage. He brought up his son Richard
on a system, and meant to marry him by
system at the age of twenty-five. Unfortunately when this scientific humanist was
away consulting family physicians and
lawyers about a helpmeet for his peerless
son, the magnetic youth sculling down the
river had his vision of the magnetic maiden ;
and, nature speaking in his bosom less sen-
tentiously than the baronet, he straightway
took his part in one of the prettiest love-
scenes in literature. Richard was only
eighteen, Lucy was a year younger ; about
the age when they ought to have been

whipped. So precisely thought Adrian
Harley, the wise youth. But when the wise
youth and the scientific humanist fought
romance with civilisation, misery came of it.
Mr. Meredith is no sentimentalist, he is indeed
our scourge for sentimentalists ; yet his heart
is surely all with Richard and Lucy. Which
is right ? Richard Feverel or the Wise
Youth ? Molière or the Magistrate ? Romance or Civilisation ?

Well, suppose for a crooked answer to
a cross question we betake ourselves to
the lavish oracle of Bulwer Lytton. Bulwer
wrote *Pelham* when he was twenty-two ; and
he represented Pelham as dominating a
brilliant and cynical society when he had
but barely left college. He wrote *Devereux*
the year after ; and Devereux concludes the
history of his life at thirty-four with the
confession that love was for him a thing of
the past. It was twelve years later before
Ernest Maltravers and its sequel *Alice* were
finished ; and the reader might gather from
those romances that though eighteen may be
the age of folly and passion, the age for true
heroism is thirty-six. Later, Lytton took

refuge in the old romantic device of an elixir of perpetual youth. At whatever age one finds one's-self, to be persuaded that *that* is the age of romance, is not this the true elixir of perpetual youth?

ON THE NAMING OF NOVELS

WHEN Wilkie Collins died, the journals told anecdotes about the straits he had sometimes found himself in for a title. He was especially perplexed, it seems, over a volume of stories, which ultimately entered the world as *Mrs. Zant and the Ghost and other Stories.* The title was not so deep as *La Recherche de l'Absolu* nor so wide as *Vanity Fair*, but it was enough,—it served.

The pious reader may think a title a matter of small consequence, a thing to be left to the end like the preface ; an accomplished book might be trusted to name itself. It is something of a shock to him to picture writers of genius racking their brains for a catching title, and then solemnly writing up to it. In practice, however, the title is often found to be a first care even with writers of genius. The name has been known to precede the novel by an interval of thirty years. Some novels have never got, and never will get, beyond the name. That is the case with *La Quiquengrogne* of Victor Hugo. The name which found its novel after thirty years of waiting was Théophile Gautier's *Le Capitaine Fracasse*. In the rich and reckless days of 1830 it was a fashion in France with literary beginners to announce on the backs of their first books an imposing list of forthcoming works; it attracted attention and gave them airs of established authorship. They would choose at random a list of high-sounding and bizarre titles in the romantic taste of the time, without being at all in a position to make good the promise or having any definite plan for the books foreshadowed. In this way had appeared on Renduel's covers, a fashionable publisher of the day, an announcement of *Le Capitaine Fracasse*. Thirty years after date Gautier took up the bill drawn by his youth on futurity, and wrote the book. There was no longer any commercial obligation to meet. People had given up asking, 'When is *Le*

Capitaine Fracasse coming out?' Most
people fancied it had come out; some had
gone the length of criticising it. But none
the less the thing was on Gautier's conscience. For thirty years, amid the thousand cares of life, on his travels, in the
ceaseless grind of journalism, he was haunted
by a remorseful memory of the unfulfilled
promise, long ago forgotten, no doubt, by all
save himself. There is an Oriental fantasy
that statues and people in pictures crowd
round the artist at the Judgment Day
clamouring for souls. Gautier had a dread
that thus he would meet Le Capitaine
Fracasse. His christening had given the
hero an inchoate spiritual existence which
craved completion, an incontestable right
to become a romance in two volumes. And
so in the fulness of time Gautier endowed
him with his two volumes and housed him,
picturesquely if uncomfortably, in the Château de la Misère. The task was not
accomplished without disturbing sentimental memories, and waking regrets for a day
that was dead and in course of being ener-
getically buried by a later literary genera-

tion. Like an architect completing an unfinished design, Gautier set himself to write *Le Capitaine Fracasse* in the fashion of 1830. He strove to forget, to shut out the uncongenial present, to live retrospectively in the *beaux jours* of romanticism. The reader will not find in these pages, Gautier pathetically observes, any political, moral or religious thesis ; no great problem is discussed, no cause argued. Gautier, you see, had lived too long into the day of M. Dumas *fils*, the son who had declined an offer from his wonderful *père prodigue* of a partnership in his magnificent business of romance manufacture. Even Flaubert, who could still talk after Gautier's own heart about art for art's sake, had but now written *Madame Bovary* ; and the art of *Madame Bovary* is another pair of shoes altogether from the art of *Le Capitaine Fracasse*. Here should be an awful example to a name not to put off its novel for thirty years.

The sober English reader may decline to accept, as a normal type in methods of novel writing, the man who flaunted the too famous red waistcoat in token of literary revolution. Will he accept Dickens ? Well,

with Dickens, too, the title was the first
necessity, the originating impulse. Till he
had fixed upon his title, he could not get
seriously to work. He was in Genoa in
1844, and had a Christmas story to write.
He had never, he said, so staggered upon
the threshold before. The subject was there,
but he had not found a title for it, or the
machinery to work it with. 'Sitting down
one morning resolute for work though
against the grain, his hand being out and
everything inviting to idleness, such a peal
of chimes arose from the city as he found
"maddening." All Genoa lay beneath him,
and up from it, with some sudden set of the
wind, came in one fell sound the clang and
clash of all its steeples pouring into his
ears again and again, in a tuneless, grating,
discordant, jarring, hideous vibration, that
made his ideas "spin round and round till
they lost themselves in a whirl of vexation
and giddiness and dropped down dead."' A
couple of days later he wrote to Forster a
letter of one sentence: 'We have heard the
chimes at midnight, Master Shallow.' A
few days later again he writes: 'It is a

great thing to have my title and see my way how to work the bells. Let them clash upon me now from all the churches and convents in Genoa. I see nothing but the old London belfry I have set them in. In my mind's eye, Horatio.' Thus it was always with Dickens when setting about a new novel. Despondency, doubts, difficulties and endless experimenting, suggesting, sifting, rejecting of titles. Then of a sudden, a title found, and he was off on the composition of the book. Never were the preliminary throes more protracted than with *David Copperfield*. Toward the end of 1848 he was making holiday at Broadstairs, his mind running on a subject. 'I have not,' he writes from there,

> 'seen Fancy write
> With a pencil of light
> On the blotter so solid commanding the sea,—

but I shouldn't wonder if she were to do it one of these days. Dim visions of diverse things are floating around me :—I must go to work head foremost when I get home.' Home he goes, yet gets no further. In February, 1849, he is in Brighton : ' A sea-fog to-day, but yesterday inexpressibly delicious. My mind running like a high sea on names—not satisfied yet though.' On February 23d he had found a title of some sort, to wit, *Mag's Diversions, Being the Personal History of Mr. Thomas Mag the Younger of Blunderstone House.* Then came a series of variations in the expository part of the title, Blunderstone House after a time becoming Copperfield House. Then came *The Personal History of Mr. David Copperfield the Younger and his Aunt Margaret.* On February 26th he sent Forster a list of six names, which may be found set out at length in the Life. Forster and Dickens's children finally determined his choice among the six, and the title once settled all is plain sailing. He went through this elaborate process with most of his titles. There were a dozen tentative titles for *Bleak House,* most of them leading off with *Tom-all-alone's,* and fourteen for *Hard Times.* It was the same with *A Tale of Two Cities.* *Martin Chuzzlewit* was Martin always; but he began as Martin Sweezleden, and became in turn Sweezleback, Sweezlewag, Chuzzletoe, Chuzzleboy, Chubblewig, Chuzzlewig, and finally Chuzzlewit. In 1855 Dickens began keeping a book of memoranda and hints for subsequent working up, which contained among other things nineteen titles for novels. Of these he used up two for Christmas stories ; another, *Nobody's Fault*, was the title first adopted for *Little Dorrit*, the actual title being only substituted just as the first number was going to the printer. *Our Mutual Friend* was another ultimately used, though there had not been wanting in the interval critics to point out its inaccuracy of language. The rest no doubt will crowd about Dickens at the Judgment Day clamouring for completion. But Dickens was never the man to quail before a gibbering shade ; he would have snapped his fingers at a poor Capitaine Fracasse. Many a hard-pressed living novelist, however, might be glad to take his liabilities off his hands. In these times, harder than the hard times of Dickens, it is something to light on a list of eligible titles going begging. Two of them, *The Children of the Fathers* and *Two Generations*, have already been absorbed by Tourguéneff's great novel, *Fathers and Sons*; another, *The Young Person*, may perhaps be thought now too serious a reality to be lightly played with; *Dust*, another of them, has been used by Mr. Julian Hawthorne.

How names and titles set Dickens's imagination to work is one of the mysteries of genius. The settled name, it may be, was just an outward sign of the inward crystallising of his hitherto floating ideas. But with Dickens's confessed experience before him, nobody can presume to say that the title is of no artistic consequence. In these days, however, of over-population in fiction, the chief difficulties are perhaps rather commercial and legal. Art may have no concern with legal and commercial considerations, but the poor artist has often more concern than enough. It is becoming every day more difficult to hit upon a striking title which has not been already used; and the more obscure the forestalling book, the more tenaciously are proprietary rights in the title insisted on. One hears of authors having been forced to change twice, or even thrice, names over which they have been rejoicing with all the pride of a first discovery ; horrid tales are even told of dummy books hastily run up for the express purpose of forestalling and wringing money out of popular writers. We shall probably live to see a corner or ring in titles. Commercially, of course, the essentials of a good title are that it should arrest attention and whet appetite. The fierceness of the struggle for life among novels is the only excuse for all the silly, forced, and far-fetched names one hears. It is the commercial importance of the title that has given publishers their generally recognised claim to have a word in the choice, and they have often intervened with effect. The excellent title *Rob Roy* was, as Lockhart tells us, the suggestion of the publisher Constable, but he had great difficulty in persuading the author. 'What,' said Scott, 'Mr. Accoucheur, must you be setting up for Mr. Sponsor too !—but let us hear it.' Constable maintained that the name of the real hero would be the best possible name for the book. 'Nay,' answered Scott, and it is an answer worth a novelist's marking, 'never let me have to write up to a

name. You well know I have generally
adopted a title that told nothing.' The
bookseller, however, persevered, and after
dinner (what magic there is in a dinner!)
Scott yielded. Nor was this the only occasion on which Constable set up for 'Mr.
Sponsor.' He disliked the title of *The Abbot*,
and would fain have had instead *The Nun-
nery* as a sequel to *The Monastery*. This time
Scott did not yield,—perhaps there was no
dinner. He, however, soothed the grumbling
Constable by accepting his suggestion that
he should introduce Queen Elizabeth into a
romance as a companion picture to the Mary
Stuart of *The Abbot*. Constable was in-
stantly ready with a title and a subject, *The
Armada*,—a title, forsooth, that told nothing
and demanded no writing up to it! Kingsley did not shrink from *Hypatia*, but he
would hardly have adventured *The Armada*
for *Westward Ho!* For an Elizabethan
novel Scott turned to a subject that had long
been a favourite with him, the tragic story of
Amy Robsart. He meant to call the novel
after the ballad, *Cumnor Hall*; but Constable
again interfered and proposed *Kenilworth*.

This, on the other hand, John Ballantyne did
not approve of, and prophesied with bad
judgment and a worse pun that the result
would be something worthy of the kennel.
Scott, good easy giant, though his instinct
for the practical no less than the literary side
of his business was worth that of a street-full
of booksellers, fell in with the suggestion of
the imperious Constable, whose vanity, according to his partner Cadell, now boiled
over so much at having his suggestion again
approved that in his high moods he used to
stalk up and down his room exclaiming, ' By
G——, I am all but the author of the
Waverley Novels! '

Yet Scott had done more wisely to
stick to his own idea. The meeting at
Kenilworth was but an episode, though it
was the episode which precipitated the
catastrophe. And the title has moreover the
disadvantage of directing attention to the
anachronism of the plot. No sensible person
is afraid of anachronism in art so long as the
art triumphs, and, as here, a fine dramatic
situation is gained ; but if the art is to
triumph, it is wiser to let the sleeping his-

torical conscience lie. Scott was fully alive
to the wisdom of this policy. Left to himself he instinctively avoids the mistake of
naming an historical novel after an historical
character or event. It is *Quentin Durward*
not *Lewis the Eleventh*, *Anne of Geierstein*,
not *Charles the Bold*; there is no hint of
Saladin or crusading Richard in the *The
Talisman* or of masquerading Richard in
Ivanhoe. Scott was obviously right. He
was writing romance, not history. To give
a purely historical title is to bargain with the
reader to give him historical treatment. To
The Armada Scott could never have con-
sented ; *Kenilworth*, depend upon it, was a
concession against his better judgment. Even
the undaunted Dumas, who tackles history
more directly and more at large than Scott
ever chose to do, calls his famous book not
after Richelieu, Mazarin, or Lewis the Four-
teenth, but after the Three Musketeers. That
is an admirable title by the way, so mysterious
and suggestive. There is always something
fascinating about numbers in titles ; and here
the title is none the less admirable that the
musketeers were in fact not three but four,

and that the fourth was the best of the bunch,
the immortal d'Artagnan. But if Constable
did Scott a bad turn over *Kenilworth*, he
made amends by getting *Herries* changed to
the high-sounding romantic name *Redgauntlet*. *Herries* would have served, but it is not
the pleasant mouthful that *Redgauntlet* is.
Indeed as the Waverley Novels are the best
of all romances, so their names are the best
of all names. *Waverley, Old Mortality, The
Heart of Midlothian,*—they are perfect.
Scott's answer to Constable put the wisdom
of the thing in a nutshell. His titles arouse
curiosity without discounting it ; they are
distinctive and appropriate, come trippingly
off the tongue and satisfy the ear, and have
withal a twang of romance about them.
Scott, of course, besides his genius, had the
advantage of coming early in the day, and
had no need to shout to make himself heard
amid the din of a crowd. Miss Austen died
only a very few years after Scott turned from
poetry to prose romance, and Lytton was
only beginning to write as the wonderful
Waverley series was drawing to a close in
stress and difficulty.

But if *Ivanhoe* is the name for romance, *Tom Jones* is the name of a novel. *Tom Jones* was not by any means a name taken at random. Fielding was quite as anxious in his day, as Thackeray and George Eliot were in theirs, to claim credit for finding and making interesting an ordinary specimen of mere flesh and blood. *Tom Jones* was a name selected to indicate two things : that the hero was not to be an antiquated hero of romance, but something far more real and substantial ; and that, though a real man, he was to be more than an individual real man —he was to be typical and significant. *Tom Jones* has many followers ; I do not refer to Lady Bellaston, but to such titles as *Tom Brown* or *Mr. Smith*. It has been thought astonishing that a novel should have contrived to subsist with such a title as *Mr. Smith*. But this was no makeshift ; it is a singularly happy title. Mr. Smith, a short, stout, grey man, middle-aged, a bachelor and rich, comes as a stranger to settle near the village of Eastworld. The vulgar genteel families of the place are distracted between the professional advantages and social disad-

vantages of calling upon him, till they discover late in the day that 'the County'
knows him. The beauty among a set of
flirting motherless sisters had given such
heart as she had to give to a snob of a soldier,
who kissed her at home and denied her in the
better houses of the neighbourhood ; but for
marriage she schemes to catch the rich
middle-aged man honoured with the friendship of eligible acquaintance. Mr. Smith,
thinking no guile, and equally grateful to
kind friends of all sorts and conditions, falls
in love with the beautiful girl, but can hardly
bring himself to believe that the prize is for
him. He thinks no scandal nor will listen to
it. And then suddenly, as the author has recently said did really happen with his proto-
type in life, on the very eve of his marriage he
died. His life and his death lift the book, as
they lifted Eastworld, out of what had otherwise been a dead level of unendurable vulgarity. The soldier and girl marry ; but with eyes
opened to see their own unworthiness and with
a ' quickened sense of the compass of human
feeling' from having once known a simple,
noble Christian gentleman, Mr. Smith.

Most novels, like this one, naturally derive their point and principle of unity from the character or career, the action or passion, of some one among their personages. And the name of that person, as Constable urged rightly enough, supplies the natural name for the book. Accordingly among the myriads of works of fiction this form of title is out and away the most common. With the exception of Jane Austen's double-barrelled alliterative titles, *Pride and Prejudice, Sense and Sensibility*, which also have not been without their influence, up to Scott's time the chief novels were named after the hero or heroine : Robinson Crusoe, Moll Flanders, Tom Jones, Amelia, Joseph Andrews,—it is a remark of Mr. Austin Dobson's that Fielding wisely finds room in the full title for Parson Adams, —Pamela, Clarissa Harlowe,—Richardson inclines to the women, Fielding to the men,— Roderick Random, Peregrine Pickle, Tristram Shandy, Evelina, Cecilia. Then, one step removed, the Vicar of Wakefield and the Man of Feeling. The proper names are amplified with expository phrases such as The Personal History, The Life and Adventures, and so forth ; a fashion to which Dickens returned, perhaps for the sake of its old-fashioned flavour, after Scott had shown a more excellent way of brevity. ' His Birth and Other Misfortunes,' the expository sub-title of, if I recollect aright, *Ginx's Baby*, might have done for Tristram Shandy except that poor Tristram's misfortunes began long before his birth. The actual title, however, *The Life and Opinions of Mr. Tristram Shandy, Gentleman*, is sufficiently diverting.

Where a book depicts a small community in which no single figure is pre-eminent, we sometimes get titles like *Villette*—a neat nickname for Brussels, *Barchester Towers*, *Middlemarch*, the last as good a title as could be invented for the book. George Eliot could not have christened it after Dorothea or Lydgate without ignoring half its contents. Let us be thankful she spared us that terrible modern form of title, ' A modern Saint Theresa.' It is indeed not always easy to determine which figure is the protagonist. So among George Eliot's characters : not one man probably in a thousand would have picked out Daniel

Deronda for the honour, such as it is, of naming that not very successful book. I am not sure that, for my part, I should have picked Adam Bede for this honour; the cast-iron man dear to feminine imagination has no charm for me. Hetty would be the sentimentalist's choice, to remind Adam and Dinah, whom George Henry Lewes had joined, that while they were enjoying their blameless lives Hetty was eating out her shallow little heart in transportation. The beauty of Hetty is as deeply felt as anything in the book; and, as Mr. Browning's Fra Lippo Lippi says,

> 'If you get simple beauty and nought else
> You get about the best thing God invents.'

There are people, however, who would have named the book after Dinah. 'The Tragedy of the Hall Farm' would have the advantage of bringing into focus Mrs. Poyser's all-conquering tongue. A critic, by the way, has found great significance in the primitive and elemental savour of the name Adam Bede. The initials A, B begin the alphabet; Adam was the first man; the venerable Bede comes decidedly early in our literature. Plain folk will probably consider such criticism ridiculous. It is a coincidence that Amos Barton begins with A and B.

For *Ivanhoe*, Thackeray in parody puts *Rebecca and Rowena*. I suppose to most readers, certainly to most male readers, Rebecca is more the heroine than Ivanhoe is the hero. Rebecca and Richard Lion-heart share the honours, and that was doubtless Scott's reason for calling the book after Ivanhoe. So in *Guy Mannering*, *The Antiquary*, *Old Mortality*, he of set purpose avoids the conventional hero.

When one begins shifting titles, one knows not where to stop,—that is always the weakness of the reformer. Would not, for example, *Le Père Grandet* be the true title for *Eugénie Grandet*? The masterly delineation of the miser is the achievement of the book. His sacrifice of his daughter serves essentially to throw him into relief. But Balzac, sacrifice being a pet subject with him, prefers always to take his title from the victim of the sacrifice; Eugénie Grandet, Le Lys dans la Vallée, Le Père Goriot. *Le Père Goriot* is a good name for a fine book;

yet I am not sure that *La Maison Vauquer*
would not fit the book even better. True,
the tragedy is the tragedy of a father sacrificed to his daughter's lust and avarice. But
the *pension* is the scene and very symbol of
his martyrdom, and the house, like the book,
has dark secrets not directly connected with
Goriot's story. In his treatment of the
Maison Vauquer, Balzac reaches romanticism
through realistic methods. This one sinister
house stands out from the houses about it
with a lurid light upon it. Picked out in
this light, the mean lodging-house reveals
itself as a centre and heart of suffering,
scheming, struggling, criminal Paris. To
make the work of the builder's hands colour
and overshadow the lives of men, to give
it a physiognomy and a soul that haunt
the imagination as of a thing alive and
purposeful,—this is a note of romanticism.
It is a function of romance to read its
appropriate legend into a tower, a ruin, a
stream, a glen,—the legend which expresses
and completes it by seizing and making
permanent its lurking and evanescent suggestiveness. Accordingly, since the era of

romanticism names of places have been almost as common in titles as names of people. The long line of early English novels named after the hero or heroine is significantly broken as early as 1765 by a story named after a haunted castle, Horace Walpole's *Castle of Otranto*. Even in the eighteenth century the romantic spirit was not left altogether without witness,— the witness baffled, only half serious, only half conscious, of the dilettante Horace Walpole and his friend, the poet Gray. The book was suggested, Walpole tells us, by a dream. 'I had thought myself in an ancient castle (a very natural dream for a head like mine, filled with Gothic story), and that on the uppermost bannister of a great staircase I saw a gigantic hand in armour.' This gigantic hand in armour was, as all readers will remember, the root of the story. Gray reported that at Cambridge the book made 'some of them cry a little, and all in general afraid to go to bed o' nights.' So here in full eighteenth century we already find the temper and furniture of later romance. *The Castle of Otranto* is the precursor of a whole fantastic procession of castles, abbeys, cathedrals, palaces and prisons, destined in later years to give their names to romance and legend. Wordsworth's influence joined to Scott's has put natural scenes and homely buildings alongside of the castles and monasteries of earlier romance. Hareton Earnshaw, Catherine Linton and Heathcliff, with their untamed Yorkshire passions, fantasies, furies, are harmonised and set off against the bleak beauty of the Yorkshire moorland scenery of *Wuthering Heights.* The first glimpse we get of Maggie Tulliver is of her standing as a child watching the mill-wheel in the Floss. (To be strictly accurate by the way, it was not the Floss but its 'tributary Ripple.') 'Maggie, Maggie,' cries her mother, 'where's the use o' any one telling you to keep away from the water? You'll tumble in and be drowned some day, an' then you'll be sorry you didn't do as mother told you.' The rushing of the Floss is her song of destiny in our ears all through the quarrel and trouble about Dorlcote Mill, till in the end the flood closes over the heads of brother

and sister reunited in death. *Sister Maggie*
George Eliot herself had called the story ;
The Mill on the Floss, (bar the slight inaccuracy, one of the perfect titles), was due
to her publisher Blackwood. *The House of
the Seven Gables* is but a dwelling-place for
the curse which doomed the Pyncheons,
generation after generation, to their choking,
bloody death. Of the whole class, perhaps
the finest instance is Victor Hugo's *Notre
Dame de Paris*. The great cathedral is a
haunting, importunate presence throughout
the romance till Frollo's fingers lose their
agonised grip on its yielding leads. And
withal it is the real and sufficient symbol of
Hugo's central idea. In his three great books,
Notre Dame, *Les Travailleurs de la Mer*, and
Les Misérables, Hugo set himself to typify
the triple tyranny against which humanity
struggles, the tyranny of superstition, the
tyranny of natural forces, and the tyranny
of human law. The great cathedral typi-
fies the tyranny of the mediæval Church,
the tyranny of its beauty and grandeur,
its morbid and grotesque imagination, its
mystery and terror. And then the irony

of such a title for the story of a graceful
innocent gipsy girl hunted to death by the
lust and hate of the consecrated servant of
a religion of pity and chastity, of our pure
and gentle Lady, Notre Dame de Paris!

That is what a great title can do. It not
only summarises and clinches; it is also
commentary and chorus. Such titles as *Le
Roi s'Amuse* or *Fromont Jeune et Risler
Aîné* are whole volumes in themselves.
Hugo was not so happy with the titles of
the other two parts of his trilogy. The title
Les Misérables is too wide for its idea. We
feel after we have done with Javert and Jean
Valjean that, as I think Mr. Bret Harte puts
it at the close of his diverting parody, there
are still plenty of miserables left.

It indeed often happens that an otherwise fine title is too wide, like an algebraical
formula for a specific problem. Thackeray
is said to have been finely elated over his
title of *Vanity Fair*; but, as a matter of
fact, *Vanity Fair* does not characterise the
scenes of Becky's triumphs and degradation
any more specially or properly than it would
characterise the rest of Thackeray's works.

It has been a custom with some French novelists to adopt a general heading for a series of novels; Balzac's *La Comédie Humaine*, for example, M. Daudet's *Mœurs Parisiennes*, M. Ohnet's *Les Batailles de la Vie*, so much scoffed at by the vivacious Gyp and others. *Vanity Fair* would have served Thackeray admirably for such a purpose, with his persistent refrain of *Vanitas Vanitatum*. Many fine titles of Balzac again have this defect of overwideness. *La Femme de Trente Ans*, *Les Illusions Perdues* (which might stand as the title for Flaubert's complete works), *Les Parents Pauvres*—La Cousine Bette and Le Cousin Pons do not exhaust the dramatic possibilities of the poor relation; or lastly that very uninviting title, which would characterise a school of novels better than a single story, *Les Petites Misères de la Vie Conjugale*. This is indeed precisely what one might expect with Balzac, because Balzac set himself, quite solemnly and in apparent good faith, to exhaust the whole of human experience in the forty little yellow volumes which a modern young man has vowed he would not give in exchange for Shakespeare. Obviously no title could be too wide to indicate the magnificent scope of such a design. Of course it must not be denied that a great novel may so seize and express a typical piece of human experience as to justify the assumption of a generic title, doing in pure fiction the kind of thing which Hamlet has done in poetic tragedy. Perhaps *Vanity Fair* is such a case. Perhaps *Madame Bovary* could bear the title *Les Illusions Perdues*. Perhaps Tourguéneff's *Fathers and Sons* justifies itself by an adequate grasp and by a typical example of the inevitable tragic clash of ideas between succeeding generations in an epoch of change.

This defect of overlapping the specific subject is one of the many vices of those detestable modern titles consisting of proverbs or quotations. Mr. Swinburne once suggested that it would be a benevolent despotism, and worthy of Matthew Arnold's ideal academy, which should make it a penal offence against literature for any writer to affix a proverb, a quotation, but above all things a line of poetry, by way of tag or title to a novel. At the best, titles like *Love me little Love me long*, *It is Never too Late to Mend*, *Red as a Rose is She*, *One Traveller Returns*, are, as Mr. Swinburne calls the first, very silly labels. They are not only awkward, they are essentially illegitimate. It is generally speaking an impertinence to use up a proverb, or a fine line of poetry of world-wide application for one's own poor bounded story. It is a sacrilege to desecrate with less choice associations a name enskied and sainted in imperishable poetry,—like Proud Maisie, for instance. It is an outrage to apply to the crude sentimentality of a Kate Chester, to use indeed for any transient love-tale of the hour, the plea rung from the great tortured heart of Othello, 'Tell them I loved not wisely, but too well,' or the cry of Romeo, when he has slain Juliet's kinsman and sees himself caught in the toils of fate, 'Oh I am Fortune's fool!' I take examples at random, meaning no disrespect to the able authors of these particular novels; but they have plenty of wit to invent better titles and leave Othello's jealousy and Romeo's love in peace.

It was Lord Lytton, I fancy, who began with *What will he do with it?* the irritating fashion of using for title an interrogative sentence. A sentence for title is almost always clumsy. A phrase, however, not in itself clumsy, nor made offensive by misapplication, may make a good title ; witness the beau. tiful name of Mr. Bret Harte's very beautiful story *Left out on Lone Star Mountain.*

If after being pelted with all these instances the reader has strength left to ask with Juliet, What's in a name? (I acknowledge that that quotation is an outrage)— my answer is, the difference between *Is he Popenjoy?* which I take to be one of the worst, and *The Scarlet Letter* which I take to be one of the very best, of all titles. Consider for a moment how perfect a title *The Scarlet Letter* is. It tells nothing, yet it tells everything. It fascinates before the book is opened, it fascinates even more powerfully after the book is closed. The whole tragedy is in the title. It is the symbol of Hester's sin, and the penalty of her sin, the isolation, and the spiritual blight. The symbol of *The Scarlet Letter* eats into the imagination of the reader as it ate into the flesh of the remorse-racked Puritan minister, till we see it everywhere in the air before our eyes, as he saw it written on the thunderous sky through the wild night when he stood distracted on Hester's scaffold. The book might have lived and prospered under another name, say *The Silence of the Rev. Arthur Dimmesdale* ; but it is surely an added perfection that it should find in its title, as it does now, its final sign and seal.

NAMES IN NOVELS

EVERY lover of Balzac knows the story of the famous search which ended in the discovery of the name Z. Marcas : how Balzac appointed Léon Gozlan to meet him in the Champs Elysées to do him an important service ; how Gozlan, racking his brain to guess what this service might be, kept the appointment on a certain wintry day of June ; how it turned out that what Balzac wanted was a name for the hero of a story he was about to contribute to the *Revue Parisienne.* In the driving rain Balzac expounded his theory of names. He must have a name, he said, that would fit his hero in every possible respect, and he had exhausted his own resources without being able to find such. Now, names could not be manufactured ; like languages, they were a natural product a growth.

'If the name exists,'—began Gozlan, zealously.

'It does exist,' Balzac broke in with solemnity.

So there was but one thing to be done, to start there and then upon a voyage of discovery. Gozlan suggested a scrutiny of the names in the streets, and they set to work at once, Balzac taking one side of the road, his friend the other. They ran, head in the air, into the passers-by, who took them for blind men. Street after street Gozlan kept calling Balzac's attention to the most appetising names. Balzac rejected them all. Thus they went from the Rue St. Honoré to the Palais Royal, through all the streets abutting on the Gardens, Rue Vivienne, Place de la Bourse, Rue Neuve Vivienne, Boulevard Montmartre :—but here Gozlan mutinied.

'It is always the same,' cries Balzac, 'Christopher Columbus deserted by his crew.'

Then, turning to entreaty, he pleaded for just as far as St. Eustache. That meant a détour through innumerable streets to the Place des Victoires, studded with magnificent

Alsatian names smacking of the Rhine.
Again Gozlan threatened to abandon Balzac
unless he made an instant choice. 'Just the
Rue du Bouloi,' urges the indefatigable discoverer; and off they go once more, until in
the last section of the interminable street the
novelist stood transfixed and quivering in
front of the name 'Marcas.'

'That will do splendidly, Marcas! My
hero's name shall be Marcas. There is everything I want in Marcas: the philosopher, the
writer, the statesman, the misunderstood
poet, Marcas implies it all!'

That was what Balzac required—a name
that would at a stroke depict and interpret
his hero, a name that should match his lot in
life, a name not tacked on at random, but
fitting naturally. Balzac insisted that the
name must answer to his hero's face, figure,
voice, his past and his future, his genius and
tastes, his passions, misfortunes, and glory.
Nothing short of that would satisfy him.

Balzac was not the only novelist thus particular about names. A touching story is
told of Flaubert and M. Zola, which I give
as I read it. 'The author of *Salammbô* was

busy on his last work and with his constitutional secretiveness had not revealed plot or characters to his friends. Zola was writing a novel at the same time, and one afternoon happened to tell Flaubert of a part allotted to a man for whom he had just found the very appropriate name of Bouvard. Flaubert turned pale and presented a picture of blank discouragement. Some days later a common friend came to Zola informing him that Flaubert was in despair; that Bouvard was precisely the name he had fixed upon for one of the characters in his own book; that it had cost him six years of research and labour to find it; that he had discovered it at last in Normandy, in a village near Yvetot, and could never hope to replace it. It was all over with him if he could no longer couple the name of Bouvard with that of Pécuchet, for together they were the keystone of the work. "Well," said Zola, gravely and sadly, after a long pause, "let him have it. But I must love him very dearly to give up such a unique and unapproachable name as Bouvard. However, it belongs to an idiot, whose sign I can read

every day from my windows." The news of
the concession was carried to Flaubert, who
immediately started to embrace and thank
his friend, fully appreciating his disinterested-
ness and frankly confessing his inability to
have done the same.'

When Flaubert was writing *l'Education Sen-
timentale*, a cousin of his wrote to ask him to
change the name of his unheroic hero Frédéric
Moreau, on the ground that there were real
Moreaus at Nogent. Absolutely impossible,
replied Flaubert. A proper name was a
matter of extreme importance in a novel, 'une
chose *capitale*' (the italics being Flaubert's).
A character could no more change his name
than the Ethiopian could change his skin.
If there happened to be real Moreaus at
Nogent, so much the worse for them.

Nor was it a bit of M. Zola's fun when he
professed to make a hard sacrifice to friendship' in resigning to Flaubert his chosen
name. Quite recently he has made in public
a confession of faith that falls not at all short
of the Balzacian and Flaubertian fanaticism.
He, too, is a fatalist in the matter of names,
firmly believing that a mysterious correlation

exists between the man and the name he
bears. What, however, with Balzac was
whim and fantasy, M. Zola after his fashion
has reduced to system. He does not roam
in the rain at hazard through the streets of
Paris,—not he! He uses a directory. There-
from he makes a list of names which strike
him as likely to prove valuable, and selects
from time to time the most appropriate for
the parts he has in hand. That M. Zola
regards as reducing nomenclature to a
'science.' More interesting is M. Zola's remark, that he judges a young author by the
names which he bestows upon his characters.
If the names strike him as weak or unsuit-
able, he loses all interest in the writer and all
belief in his capacity. For a dissonance
between a name and a character he regards
in a novel as a very grave defect.

I suppose all novelists and story-tellers,
whether or not they are so exacting as this,
take some proper godfatherly or godmotherly
care in the christening of their creatures.
If they go no deeper, they at least observe
the more superficial and obvious distinctions
between character of bourgeois and gentle

blood. They seek names appropriate to calling or locality, and so forth. Most take some pains at least about the naming of hero and heroine. One class of novelists appeals to a sentiment of romance with high-sounding, historic names; another betrays the inevitable significance of nomenclature by scrupulously employing none but the most familiar. For myself, I own I like my lady-loves of romance to have names that the lips and the memory can linger over lovingly,—Lorna Doone, Lucy Desborough, Di Vernon, Beatrix Esmond. Clare Doria Forey is like the close of a rich hexameter, Mr. Lang has said. Poor Clare liked to write her name so in full, because her cousin's name was Richard Doria Feverel. Nothing short of democratic training and Bostonian naturalism could have hardened Mr. Howells's heart into inflicting upon his Lady of the Aroostook and her many admirers, for the sake of whatever dramatic point, the revolting surname Blood. Beautiful and picturesque names are no small element in the picturesque beauty of romance. We revel in a luxury of graceful names in

Arthur's court—amongst the Guineveres, and
and Iseults, and Tristrams, and Launcelots.
They have the flavour of fruit on the lips,
and haunt the ear like music. Generations
of hearts have beaten time to the syllables
Wilfred of Ivanhoe or Lucy of Lammermoor. The degradation of name is a bit
brutal, even for parody, in the diverting
'Rejected Address' which transforms—

> ' " Charge, Chester, charge ! On, Stanley, on ! "
>   Were the last words of Marmion,'

into

> ' " 'Od rot 'em,"
>   Were the last words of Higginbottom.'

Juliet was the daughter of a land of lovely
names, or she would never have asked her
hackneyed question. To northern ears the
vowelled Italian names all sound beautiful
and magnificent. One wonders, ignorantly
no doubt, how an Italian Dickens would
find himself in droll and grotesque names.
There must be some temptation to make all
the boobies and villains Germans. Thanks
to what Matthew Arnold termed the touch
of grossness in our race, we are bounti-
fully provided with names of all shades of
vulgarity and hideousness. With us no

booby nor villain, at all events, need go
inappropriately named. But it is unpardonable in fiction to burden a charming girl
with a vile name, and to make heroes of
Higginbottoms is a mere wantonness of
Zolaism. Art exists to console us for the
hardships and anomalies of life.

Glaring offences most writers avoid. They
succeed in securing at all events the superficial proprieties of nomenclature. But what
Balzac sought was a propriety of nomenclature going very much deeper than this.
He was a believer in a mysterious affinity
and reciprocal influence between names and
people in actual life. Philosophers and the
mob, he claimed, were at one in holding this
view, so that there was no room left for a
single heretic without the pale.

'Except for me,' interjected Gozlan.

What!—didn't Gozlan believe that there
were names which recalled special objects—
a sword, a flower? that there were names
which at once veiled and revealed the poet,
the philosopher, the painter? Racine, for
example—the very name, surely, depicted a
tender passionate poet.

On the contrary, said Gozlan, to him it only suggested a botanist or an apothecary.

'Well, Corneille? Corneille?'

No; from Corneille the stubborn heretic got simply the idea of some insignificant bird. And, unconverted, he joined, as a sheer act of good-fellowship, in the Columbus expedition, without a shred of faith in the promised land. Nor, it must be confessed, was his scepticism shaken even by the superb discovery, which intoxicated the romance-writer. Balzac, equally unshaken, carried the courage of his conviction to the pitch of fearlessly guaranteeing actually at the man's door that the veritable Marcas would turn out to be a genius, a Benvenuto Cellini.

'Wasn't that going rather far?' hinted Gozlan.

'With a name like that,' comes the sturdy reply, 'it is impossible to go too far.'

The real Marcas was a tailor. Balzac's head drooped for a few seconds. In a moment it was proudly raised again. 'The man deserved a better lot,' he said; 'anyway, it should be his business to immortalise him.'

Respectable authority might be quoted in support of Balzac's dogma from the days of the solemn naming and renaming amongst the Hebrews, down to the opinion of the immortal Mr. Shandy. But whether we accept it, or feel inclined rather to range ourselves with the Gozlanites, there can be little doubt that, in fiction at all events, there should be some subtle appropriateness in the naming of the *dramatis personæ*.

What should be the nature of the appropriateness? What should be the secret of the affinity? Should novelists permit themselves to manufacture names of transparent significance, such as Fielding's Allworthy, to take one of the early and simplest instances? Or, like Balzac, ought they to search for mystic meanings in real names? Or ought they to avoid significant names altogether? In the first place, can there possibly be any affinity, apart from association, between a mere meaningless proper name and a character? Gozlan said No. He accounted for the significance that Balzac found in such names as Racine and Corneille, by the fact that they had been borne by

those great men. The characteristics of the
poets had become associated in the mind
with the sound of the names. This is no
doubt largely true. The influence of association in matters of this kind is astonishingly
powerful, and it is an influence difficult to
discount. Of such associations of ideas
have not philosophers been found to create
worlds and systems, which they have themselves pronounced to be very good? Take
such names as Keats and Chaucer, for
example. Would they not sound poor and
mean, could we once rob them of their
associations? And the influence of association is all the stronger in the case of the
men and women in novels, because we know
them so much more intimately than we
know our friends and neighbours in real
life.

Chadband, Miss Miggs, Micawber, Pecksniff, Sairy Gamp — were these names,
then, really once absolutely non-significant?
Surely, in the mere name of Micawber there
already lurk suggestions of a waiting for
something to turn up. Enthusiasts have
been known to protest that from Silas

Wegg's bare name they divined the whole man, wooden leg and all.

Not a bit of it, retorts rationalising common-sense; make the experiment in a properly scientific spirit, and see. Set a man innocent of Dickens to evolve from the letters of the word Pecksniff the character of the Salisbury architect, or from the data of a misshapen body and sly domestic cruelty ask him to construct the name Quilp.

Well, and suppose he fail, his failure is by no means fatal to the theory. To begin with, nature undoubtedly affords abundant instances of mysterious affinities between apparently heterogeneous things. There is the story, constantly told by psychologists, of the blind man who, on his receiving his sight by a surgical operation, straightway pro-nounced scarlet to be like the sound of a trumpet. Heliotrope owes its popular name to a curious identity of scent and taste. Novel-readers who follow the fashion may recall the passage in one of those Russian novels which are twice as natural as life, where the capricious child Natacha tries to explain to her mother in bed how she thinks of her lover Boris as being quite narrow and pale grey, whereas Bésoukhow was blue, dark blue and red, and made her think of a square thing. In very truth, scents, sounds, and colours have infinite capacities of spiritual suggestion. Herein lies the secret of the potency of the sensuous arts.

What analysis could exhaust the possible suggestiveness of names? There are forebodings in the mere sound of the syllables, and mysterious intimations in the mere look of the letters, which baffle all attempts at rational explanation. And on this groundwork association has woven intricate threads of suggestion, philological, historical, romantic. Then, additional effect is wrought by a subtle conjunction of names. Trace the associations in the two names, Clive, Newcome. Watch how the music of Ethel Newcome's name is troubled into discord by prefixing to the surname the monosyllable Barnes. Nonsense, interrupts common-sense. The monosyllable Clive had served just as well to trouble the music, if Thackeray had but distributed the parts differently, and made Barnes a hero. It is all the effect of associating man and name together.

Well, but how comes it, then, that in so many names, in spite of association, we do not feel the affinity? To this day I am persuaded that Arabin was only an assumed name of the Dean of Barchester. Other names, again, there are which answer only to a part of the character. In Hetty Sorrel's name, for example, there is the kittenish grace and rustic charm ; but where is the hard heart and vulgar vanity of Martin Poyser's niece? (Poyser, by the way, is an excellent name for that admirable couple.) And poor Major Dobbin's foolish name leaves out the gallantry and loyalty, preserving only and accentuating the notion of a certain thick-hided patience. If Balzac's faith ran something near to fanaticism, yet, so far as fiction is concerned, it is surely founded on wisdom. It is true that it is only after name and character have been joined together by the inspiration of the author that they cannot again be put asunder ; but the marriage only reveals, and does not beget, the elective affinity. There is a similar revelation of affinity, in spite of Schopenhauer's dogmatic utterance to the

contrary, when music is married to immortal
verse by a composer of dramatic genius.
Common-sense would scarcely evolve Schumann's melody from Heine's *Ich grolle
nicht*, or Heine's poetry from Schumann's
music ; yet that marriage of music and
verse was none the less surely made in
heaven.

Oftentimes, however, either there has been
lacking the genius to create or discover
names of the miraculous potency of Z. Marcas, or novelists have lacked faith in the
discernment of their readers ; and recourse
has been had to manufactured names with
obvious meanings. Dickens, who had a
wonderful faculty for creating or discovering,
at all events for his ludicrous or vulgar
characters, droll and *bizarre* names of startling aptness, has given us also Lord Frederick
Verisopht, Sir Mulberry Hawk, Dotheboys
Hall, and a multitude of like inventions.
How far is this a legitimate practice ? There
are people who go into ecstasies of admiration over the ingenuity and wit displayed in
the invention of names like these. There
are others who scornfully condemn the

device as a symptom of poverty of imagination or mistaken art. Most readers, I fancy, will find themselves differently affected by different examples. Many a reader will be startled and offended by Wrench and Filgrave as names for doctors in George Eliot and Trollope, who would have an easy tolerance for Lord Frederick Verisopht, and would positively enjoy Jingle and the Veneerings. For myself, I revel in the Deuceaces and Barcacres, whereas it is a relief to me that Becky so soon merges her too significant surname in that of poor Rawdon Crawley.

Upon reflection, the different judgments would seem to be due to no irrational caprice of taste. The kind of name felt to be appropriate depends upon the author's method of presenting his creatures. No sane reader quarrels with the Fidessas and Duessas, the Sansfoys and Sansloys of the *Faerie Queene*. Every reader of sense derives the keenest satisfaction from the names of the diverting population of Bunyan's Vanity Fair—Sir Having Greedy, my Lord Fair-speech, and Mr. Facing-both-ways, Mr. Love-lust and Mr. Live-loose, Mr. Heady and Mr. High-

mind. The reason is clear. Here we are in
a world of allegory. The aim is to teach
the reader, not to take him in with a show of
reality. Here we are only one step removed
from the old miracle-play, with its abstract
virtues and vices brought on to the stage
without any pretence of substantial personifi-
cation. Bunyan's narrative may beguile us
till we follow the combat between Christian
and Apollyon with a zest like that with
which we watch one of d'Artagnan's feats of
swordsmanship, or Jan Ridd's prowess with
his fists; yet all the while we remain aware
that Christian is not a man, but a personified
type.

Let us go a step nearer to the novel. Of
the motley crowd who people the English
comic stage, a large proportion are signed in
the forehead with these directly significant
names—from Madge Mumblecrust and Tibet
Talkapace of *Ralph Roister Doister*, down
to the Surfaces, Teazles, Crabtrees, Backbites,
Absolutes and Languishes of Sheridan, to
come no later. What a world to live in,
were it real! Carlyle had a vision of an
unclothed world, where the robes should fall

from king and courtier, leaving only so many
forked radishes, with heads fantastically
carved. But the ensuing chaos would be
order compared with this world of exposed
souls. The commerce of life would be at a
standstill. What way could be found of
being genial with Morose or confidential with
Sir Giles Overreach, or with what countenance should we introduce Sir Amorous la
Foole to the ladies of our family? We should
have to stuff our handkerchiefs down our
throats on being gravely introduced to Sir
Fopling Flutter and Major Oldfox, unless,
perchance, unseasonable mirth were checked
by the reflection that our own style and title
had to be given in exchange as Dame Pliant
or Sir Epicure Mammon. Why do not such
absurdities, such patent unrealities, mar our
interest in the great comedies? Simply
because the world of the comic stage is not,
nor is it presented as, the everyday world of
decently disguised souls and bodies. This
very unreality, the making transparent of
opaque realities, is a chief element in the
delightfulness of the comic drama. 'The
Comic Spirit,' says Mr. Meredith, in his

introductory remarks to *The Egoist*, 'has not
a thought of persuading you to believe in
him. Being a spirit, he hunts the spirit in
men : vision and ardour constitute his merit.'
It is chiefly in his comedy characters that Mr.
Meredith allows himself the use of such
significant names as that 'masterpiece of
scientific nomenclature,' Sir Willoughby Pat-
terne. For comedy we settle ourselves in
our seats and adjust our opera-glasses, and
lay ourselves out to extract the uttermost
measure of critical amusement from the
sayings and doings of the cleverly constructed
world beyond the footlights. Illusion of
reality is not sought. Significant names are
a part of the game, like the other conventions
of the stage, from soliloquy to rouge and
powder. They have many special advantages in comedy. They do for the comic
dramatist what a well-known story did for
the ancient tragedians, or for Shakespeare in
his historical plays,—they give to the gestures
and speeches of the actors pungency of irony
and piquancy of revelation. But a comedy
must be something more than an allegory.
There must be a counterbalancing measure

of realism. The comic dramatist must make you so far take his *dramatis personæ* for men and women, as to enable you to sympathise with their feelings and lose yourself in their fortunes. A proper regard for young Absolute will not allow us to remember too rigorously Lydia's disparaging maiden name; and we are glad to be beguiled by the realistic touch given by old Absolute that she was not one of the Languishes of Worcestershire, but was the Miss Languish who came with her aunt, Mrs. Malaprop, into their country just before Jack was last ordered to his regiment.

According as the element of allegory or the element of realism predominate in the artist's method, will be the wisdom or un-wisdom of employing realistic or allegorical names. Where allegory predominates, where our attention is directed chiefly to the skill of the dramatist in showing up the foibles of humanity, and winding mean and vicious actions into situations of laughable entangle-ment, then names which point the character and explain situation come naturally in place. But where it is sought to stir pity and fear and sympathy with the sufferings and heroisms of men and women ; where, as in tragedy, self-conscious observation of the writer's art should be lost in overwhelming feeling for the hero's destiny, there, so far as I know, such names have never been adopted. Ben Jonson, much of whose work is, as Mr. Swinburne has recently said, a study not of humanity but of humours, uses significant names almost exclusively in his comedies. Shakespeare, on the other hand, is sparing in his use of them. Justices Shallow, Slender, and Silence, with Fang and Snare the sheriff's officers—the majesty of the law always fares badly in the hands of satire ; the constable, Dull ; Froth, a foolish gentleman ; Martext, a vicar ; and that ragged regiment of Falstaff's recruits, Mouldy, Shadow, Wart, Feeble, and Bullcalf,—almost exhaust the list.

Have we not here the explanation of the instinctive shock which we feel on being introduced by George Eliot or Trollope to the doctors, Wrench and Filgrave ? We are taking Middlemarch and the Middlemarchers in perfect seriousness and good faith. We

know the people well, and understand their
life ; we need no prompting to divine the jar
between the old humdrum practitioners and
Lydgate with his modern science. To be
told that the humdrum practitioner is named
Wrench or Filgrave is like receiving a slap
in the face. We are rudely awakened, the
illusion of reality is brusquely dispelled. The
names are so glaringly made up ; it is too
unnatural to find these names crying in the
wilderness, preparing in the medical desert
of Middlemarch a highway for a truer
science. Where the aim is to produce by
art an illusion of everyday reality, where the
artist desires to keep himself and his artistic
scaffolding entirely out of sight, or only pre-
sents himself for the purpose of commenting
on people and things which are supposed to
exist independently of him, then the flinging
in the reader's face of palpably manufactured
names is the unpardonable sin of art, inconsistency. It is not to be pleaded that names
of this kind do actually occur in real life,
sometimes with startling appropriateness.
That truth is stranger than fiction, it has
been said, is but another way of saying that

fiction may not dare to be so strange as
truth. And the cleverest disciple of perhaps
the greatest master of legitimate naturalism
in fiction admitted that the realists should
rather call themselves illusionists, and must
abstain from reproducing what is startling in
reality. In George Eliot's case the explanation would seem to be, that she adopted significant names for the small parts, to serve
instead of the long description which they
would not bear ; just as at the end of the
list of *dramatis personæ*, instead of 'serving-
men,' 'sheriff's officers,' or a more unsavoury
retinue, the playwright sometimes puts 'Fang,
Snare,' etc. But, however legitimate for the
playwrights, it is a practice really inadmissible
in works like *Middlemarch* or Trollope's
novels. There, small as the point is, it is a
flaw. It makes the art obtrusive just where
it should remain concealed ; it wakes the
reader's suspicious criticism, just where such
criticism should be lulled to sleep. It is a
reappearance, in the least *naïve* of the arts, of
those scrolls which issue so naïvely out of
the mouths of the personages in old pictures.

It is not difficult to see with how much

more of natural case Dickens can introduce
his Jingles and Veneerings. The art of
Dickens is often the art of caricature, often
it is the art of farce. His world is a grotesque, pathetic, lurid, ludicrous world of his
own. He has brought together a teeming
population of quacks and mountebanks, and
waifs and strays, and monstrosities, for whom
his most extravagant names are accepted as
the only natural and proper ones. Another
reason, no doubt, that many of his names fit
the people with such convincing exactitude
is simply that the people themselves have as
little of a third dimension as the names. In
his wonderful art Dickens found room for
characters that are hardly characters at all
—not men and women, that is to say,
but rather phantasms, admirably suited to
heighten the effect of his *mise-en-scène*;
phantasms that crack their finger-joints like
Newman Noggs, or play some other pantomime which will add just the ghastly, or
droll, or *bizarre* tone which he needs for his
effect.

But what shall we say of Thackeray and
his Deuceaces and Barcacres and the rest?

Thackeray is verily as great a realist as a great artist can be. He prides himself on presenting life as it is, unseasoned by the hot spices of artificial romance. Nay he employs devices to entrap the credulity of the reader—the device, for example, of making Arthur Pendennis, whom we know independently, tell the story of his young friend Clive Newcome, and the noble meek-hearted gentleman with whom he had seen the boy at the Cave of Harmony. His characters are no decorative figments to amuse our fancy. They have become some of the men and women we know best, personal friends or foes of our own. It consoles us for living in these late days of a reformed Parliament, that we have lived late enough to have known Colonel Newcome. They are no tears of unreal sentiment that we weep over his martyrdom ; it is a very genuine itch we feel to kick Barnes. In Thackeray's case the justification of the artificial names lies in this, that with all the solid reality of the life portrayed, we are never allowed to lose sight of the author and his art in portraiture. He is ever at hand to underline the snobbery or laugh off the pathos. The strain of the satirist is strong in him, and satire is akin to allegory; there is even a strain of the caricaturist ready to emerge in the midst of his noblest art. He is especially fond of putting on the airs and graces of the showman. His preface to *Vanity Fair* is headed 'Before the Curtain'; and this great novel of real life concludes with 'Come, children, let us shut up the box and the puppets, for our play is played out.' And we accept Thackeray's showman's humour. He chooses to treat a character as a puppet and call it Deuceace—that is his whim; we know the man, and believe in him none the less. We are not to be taken in with the made-up name. ' The famous little Becky puppet,' he wrote, ' has been pronounced to be uncommonly flexible in the joints and lively on the wire.' No: for my part, I cannot allow Thackeray himself to treat Mrs. Rawdon Crawley as a mere puppet; and that I think is why I resent her artificial maiden name.

THE HISTORICAL NOVEL

THE historical novel has never found favour with the unco critical, nor is their hostility without certain obvious justification. It is a matter of common observation how sadly writers err the moment they leave the sphere of their personal experience. The male novelist, who is wise, shuns the details of his heroine's dress, and, like Mr. Black, contents himself with such safe generalities as 'all in cream white with a bunch of scarlet geraniums in her bosom.' The light brigade of lady novelists, less easily daunted, makes its heroic charge into university slang and the secrets of the smoking-room ; and we exclaim, '*C'est magnifique*,' but we do not look for success. If the pitfalls lie so close at our door, to plunge into the dim distances of history must surely be to court disaster. And when, instead of considering probabilities, we turn to examples of novels historical and unhistorical by the same authors, it may seem to some that a comparison of, say, *Romola* with *Adam Bede*, or of *Esmond* with *The Newcomes*, goes to support the view of the critics. In spite of the subtle truth of the picture of moral dissolution presented in Tito, most people in reading *Romola* experience a chilling sense of general unreality, and withal a fatiguing consciousness of the author's effort to be accurately Florentine, which prevents it from taking in their hearts an equal place with the earlier stories of middle-class English life. *Esmond* is a favourable example for the author: the age of Queen Anne is not very far removed from to-day, and the pages of *The Spectator* make its character and manners familiar; Thackeray had an intimate literary knowledge of it—indeed Professor Seeley has had to combat the heresy that the novelist would have been its best historian. Yet *Esmond* even, compared with *Vanity Fair* or *The Newcomes*, has suffered somewhat in popularity from its constraint of pose. Nay, take Scott himself. Few will dissent from

the opinion that Scott's strongest characters
are to be found among the types he knew,
the peasants and lairds and bailies of
Scotland and the Border, the immortal race
of Dandie Dinmonts and Nicol Jarvies.
That was Lockhart's opinion. For the
matter of that, it was Scott's own opinion.
You may set Isaac of York and Rebecca
beside Davie and Jeanie Deans, without
any loss of picturesque charm, but hardly
without some weakening of the sense of
their reality.

No sooner had the prestige of Scott's
triumph waned, and his wand fallen into the
hands of weaker wizards, impotent to work his
spells, than critical objections to historical
romance began to find vigorous expression.
The hostility of the professed historians
was no doubt to be expected. But there is
Mr. Leslie Stephen, a professed literary
critic, who has spoken in his time much
good sense about fiction, frankly giving up
the historical novel. *Hypatia* and *Westward Ho!* he speaks of as brilliant but
almost solitary exceptions to the general
dreariness of their class. He is sure they are

full of hopeless inaccuracies : he does not believe that men like the Goths ever existed in this world ; and he is prepared to give up the whole tribe of monks, pagans, Jews, and Fathers of the Church. Even in his 'dear *Ivanhoe*' he thinks that the buff-jerkin business, which aroused Carlyle's easily aroused contempt, is an element of decay, and that consequently the book is on the high road to ruin, like one of Reynolds's most carelessly painted pictures. He quotes with approval Sir Francis Palgrave's opinion, that historical novels are the mortal enemies of history ; and adds for himself that they are mortal enemies of fiction. 'There may be an exception or two, but as a rule the task is simply impracticable. The novelist is bound to come so near to the facts that we feel the unreality of his portraits.' This is plain speaking ; yet in spite of all this Mr. Stephen confesses that he rejoices in the Amal and Raphael ben Ezra, and that he loves Ivanhoe and Front-de-Bœuf and Wamba the Witless.

If the lover chastise thus with whips, it were no wonder if the late Professor

Freeman and the Bishop of Oxford chastised
with scorpions. Yet was it with some
evident lingering tenderness for the romance
that Freeman in a certain lecture admonished
the undergraduate anxious to understand
the age of the Crusades to forbear, 'if he
could so steel himself,' from reading *Ivanhoe*.
Objections, however, from the point of view
of the tutor of history are not necessarily
valid objections in the sphere of artistic
criticism. There are no doubt occasions
when the tutor, like the British matron,
may have a word to say on artistic
questions. But my inquiry is not whether
these romances are good science, but whether
they are good art ; and historical inaccuracy
will only concern me if it spoil the novel
as a novel, if it weaken, that is, the interest
of the story or the force of the dramatic
passion. It is no part of the proper function
of art to impart information ; and the
judicious novel-reader will rather rejoice
that his 'dear *Ivanhoe*' is of no use for the
schools. If it is to be read at all, let it be
read, not for the sake of some illegitimately
acquired information, but for its own sake,

that the reader, like Mr. Stephen, may love Wilfred, and Front-de-Bœuf, and Wamba the Witless; that he may shudder when Rebecca stands on the dizzy edge that sunders death from dishonour; and in spite of the scoff of the humourist breathe a sigh of honest relief, when the Templar, 'unscathed by the lance of the enemy falls a victim to the violence of his own contending passions.'

In considering the strictures on historical novels, the first thing that strikes one is, that similar objections might be made as well to most poetical treatments of historical subjects. An undergraduate who should boast, like the great Duke of Marlborough, that he had learnt all his history from Shakespeare, would, there can be no doubt, have fared as badly at Freeman's hands as he who had pinned his simple faith to *Ivanhoe* or *The Talisman*. Wonderfully as Shakespeare's *Julius Cæsar* has caught from Plutarch the spirit of an epoch so different from Elizabethan England, it manifestly would not bear the microscope of modern research. Yet poetry is freely allowed the licence which is, it seems, to be denied to the novel. There are indeed not wanting signs of a tendency on the part of science to dispute this license in the case of poetry also. But hitherto at all events there has been a clear difference between the attitude of criticism to the historical novel, and its attitude to historical plays or poems in respect of this matter of accuracy. Poetry has been freely allowed to use all history as her storehouse of raw material, and to re-create after her fashion its heroes and heroines in her own image. Indeed a great part of our finest literature is thus derived. This difference of attitude can hardly be accidental. It must be due to an instinctive feeling in the minds of some readers at all events that the novels are spoiled by the inaccuracy, while the poetry is not. And this would imply some essential difference between the methods of poetry and the novel.

The distinction that immediately occurs to one is that, while poetry comes to us offering itself frankly as ideal re-creation, novels present themselves professedly as narratives of fact. The novel is bound to

be natural, that is, to present its facts in
their every-day guise. The reality looked
for in the poem is truth and consistency of
conception; but an illusion of literal con-
formity to fact is instinctively required of
the novel. 'Your Shakespeare fashions his
characters from the hearts outwards; your
Scott fashions them from the skin inwards,
never getting near the hearts of them.' So
wrote Carlyle, himself an unrivalled painter
of men from the skin outwards, in his essay
on the creator of Nicol Jarvie and Jeanie
Deans. Whatever one may think of Carlyle's grudging estimate of Scott, this remark
at least suggests a real contrast between the
procedure of poetry and the novel. Life as
we actually live it from day to day and from
hour to hour is, nine-tenths of it, a matter of
physical need and outward circumstance:
we eat and drink and sleep, and clothe
ourselves and house ourselves, and keep on
such terms as we may with our neighbours.
All this matter of habitual routine poetry
excludes, as irrelevant to the real import of
life, selecting only what is alive with purpose
and passion, what gives life its significance

and distinction. The novelist's method is different, though his aim is the same. His method is to present his subject in its every-day dress to the every-day apprehension. He accordingly is bound to wrap his drama in a web of incidents and conversation which shall mimic the routine of every-day life.

George Eliot's *Adam Bede*, like the episode of Gretchen in Goethe's *Faust*, is a tragedy of seduction. In the poetry, each of the Gretchen scenes stands out by itself, essential and significant. The story of Hetty Sorrel, in the novel, on the other hand, is completely wrapped up in the daily life of the old English village—church-going and methodist preaching, Adam's carpentering and Mrs. Poyser's butter-making and all. For Gretchen's soul there is visible victory of the angels of light over Mephistopheles. Hetty Sorrel is convicted and transported. The old grandfather grumbles in the chimney corner, 'I mun begin to be looked down on now, an' me turned seventy-two last St. Thomas's, an' all the under-bearers and pall-bearers as I 'n picked for my funeral are i' this parish and the next to 't. It 's o' no use now. I mun be ta'en to the grave by strangers.' And Adam, Hetty's lover, marries Dinah, the methodist preacher.

Le Père Goriot has been well called a French *Lear*. Both are tragedies of the cruelty of ungrateful daughters. Lear is the typical tragedy on that theme for all time. *Le Père Goriot* is an extremely Parisian tragedy. It is curious to note with the parallelism of conception the contrast of method between the unthroned Lear with his dwindling body-guard, and old Goriot exiled from home, driven by degrees from the first floor to the garret in his lodging-house. We divine Lear's degradation by Lear's rage. We divine Goriot's sufferings from our intimate acquaintance with the hideous daily life at the Maison Vauquer, down to the lodging-house smell of the dining-room, and the slang of his fellow-lodgers.

This difference of method accounts—does it not?—for a large measure of the special difficulties of the historical novel. To realise how abundant and convincing is the familiar detail habitually employed in

novels like these of Balzac and George Eliot,
is to realise the hopelessness of the task
of the writer who should set about to do
the same thing for the age of the Crusades.
It is just because George Eliot conscien-
tiously endeavoured to do for Florence, for
Savonarola and Tessa, what she did for
Hayslope, for Mr. Irwine and Mrs. Poyser
and Hetty that the book is the comparative
failure that it is. It is not merely that such
details are beyond the reach of an archæo-
logy more searching than any novelist can
attempt. Even if learning could supply
the medieval analogue of every detail in
Adam Bede, it would be of no use, because
neither the writer nor the reader of to-day
would have the necessary instinctive feeling
of its dramatic significance. The modern
novelist uses his wealth of modern detail
intuitively, in a sense unconsciously, feeling
immediately and without effort its dramatic
effect, indeed feeling the dramatic passion
in and by means of the detail. Such
tragedies as *Adam Bede* and *Le Père
Goriot* are born incarnate in the minds of
a Balzac or a George Eliot. Similarly the

reader immediately and without effort takes
in along with the details their full significance. In the historical novel this is
impossible. 'Either,' to quote Mr. Leslie
Stephen once more, 'the novel becomes
pure cram, a dictionary of antiquities dis-
solved in a thin solution of romance, or,
which is generally more refreshing, it takes
leave of accuracy altogether.' And there is
a subtler difficulty. Sentiment—and a novel
must deal largely with sentiment—changes
rapidly. A writer of to-day can no more
put his spirit back some centuries than a
man of fifty can feel like a boy of fifteen.
And in this matter of accurate sentiment,
as in the matter of accurate detail, there is
the reader to be considered. If it were
possible to reproduce the sentiment of a
bygone time, accuracy would be dearly
purchased by the sacrifice of dramatic im-
pressiveness and of the reader's sympathy.
Scott, in the dedicatory epistle to Dr. Dry-
asdust prefixed to *Ivanhoe*, shows himself
fully alive to this, and as an artist deliberately puts dramatic interest above historical
accuracy.

'It is true,' he writes, 'that I neither can
nor do pretend to the observation of complete accuracy, even in matters of outward
costume, much less in the important points
of language and manners. But the same
motive which prevents my writing the
dialogue of the piece in Anglo-Saxon or
Norman-French, and which prohibits my
sending forth to the public this essay
printed with the types of Caxton or
Wynken de Worde, prevents my attempt-
ing to confine myself within the limits of
the period in which my story is laid. It is
necessary for exciting interest of any kind
that the subject assumed should be, as it
were, translated into the manners, as well
as the language, of the age we live in. No
fascination has ever been attached to Oriental literature equal to that produced by Mr.
Galland's first translation of the Arabian
tales ; in which, retaining on the one hand
the splendour of Eastern costume, and on
the other the wildness of Eastern fiction, he
mixed these with just so much ordinary
feeling and expression, as rendered them
interesting and intelligible.'

There is the common-sense of the matter in a nutshell.

Clearly, then, the historical novel has very definite negative limitations. But to admit thus much is by no means to give it up altogether, as Mr. Leslie Stephen has sorrowfully brought himself to do. A criticism which is bound by its theory to say that *Ivanhoe* and *Les Trois Mousquetaires* are not good novels surely stands self-condemned. The keenest admirer of the art which has given us *Eugénie Grandet*, *Madame Bovary*, or *Amos Barton* will occasionally, when in the swing of Dumas's stride, and under the spell of his matchless buoyancy and resource, recall those masterpieces with something like a mental yawn. Scott and Dumas have fascinated and continue to fascinate thousands who are perfectly well aware that the history of their novels is as romantic as the fiction. Whatever else it may do, the inevitable inaccuracy, which, as we see, Scott serenely admits, manifestly does not spoil the novel as a novel for the unsophisticated reader. He instinctively recognises that he has to do

with a different kind of novel, depending for
its effect upon different conditions. To
confound the kinds, and require the same
conditions in all, is but a blundering criticism.

If *Le Père Goriot* is worthy to be called
a French *Lear*, *Les Trois Mousquetaires*
may not unfitly be styled a French *Iliad*.
Scott and Dumas were in fact born story-
tellers, and story is not tied down to rigorous
scientific accuracy. It depends upon a sense
of beauty, rather than on a demand for
truth : its appeal is to the imagination.
Like much beautiful Oriental decoration it
may set literal truth at defiance, yet convince
by its decorative propriety. When we read
these romances, we are not studying archæo-
logy, nor are we looking for solutions of
psychological or moral problems : we simply
ask to be interested by the story, and
charmed by romantic scenes and stirring
incidents. We demand before all things
beauty and imaginative satisfaction. We
crave a poetic justice, which would be
childish in the other sphere : heroism must
triumph and villainy die the death. And

provided the imagination be satisfied, literal accuracy is immaterial. In order to satisfy the imagination, the novelist, it is true, must produce a temporary illusion of reality ; but it is enough if the spirit be cheated or charmed into acquiescence. In a recent book on Shakespeare it was laid down as a canon of dramatic criticism, that improbability only apparent to subsequent reflection was no valid objection to a piece of action felt by an actual spectator to be at the time natural and right. Now the magic of these masters of narrative fiction produces at the time just the illusion of reality appropriate to their class and scale of work. While you surrender yourself to their spell you feel yourself moving naturally among historic scenes and personages. While you have faith, you walk the treacherous waters like the firm earth. The interest and charm prevent your being disquieted by critical doubts at the time, whatever history may have to say to you on the morrow when you are in cold blood. And illusion is rendered the easier to produce by the kind of detail and scale of character-drawing appropriate to what we may call the epic novel. Minute and elaborate character and familiar detail are here out of place. Yet it is a grave mistake to suppose character and incident independent of each other, much less antagonistic. They are strictly inseparable: being indeed, if the expression be tolerable, statical and dynamical aspects of the same facts. We may talk of this novel being saved by its drawing of character, and that story by its plot or incidents; but true salvation lies in the right artistic proportion between character and incident. The incidents, for after all they are incidents, of *Eugénie Grandet* and *Madame Bovary* are just the inevitable incidents in the evolution of the moral tragedy. So, on the other hand, there is in fact admirable drawing of character in Athos, Porthos, and Aramis, above all in the incomparable d'Artagnan ; but it is of the precise scale fitted to carry the rush of exciting incident. The truth of this may be recognised by imagining the effect on the narrative of replacing these splendid fellows by some of Mr. Henry James's carefully analysed souls ; but, be it

also observed, we should equally destroy
the interest of the narrative by replacing
them with the wooden lay-figures of inferior
craftsmen. If Dumas's people were mere
lay-figures, we should no longer listen with
rapture to the click and clash of d'Artagnan's sword, nor follow the progress of
Aramis's subterranean intrigues with breath-
less interest, nor weep salt tears, as all right-
minded people now do, over the Homeric
death of Porthos. An historical novelist
can only attempt elaborate character or
familiar detail on peril of awakening a fatal
critical spirit by inevitable modernisms. He
is, however, in no way obliged to incur this
peril. As Scott says in the Epistle to Dry-
asdust, our ancestors 'had "eyes, hands,
organs, dimensions, senses, affections, passions"; were "fed with the same food, hurt
with the same weapons, subject to the same
diseases, warmed and cooled by the same
winter and summer" as ourselves'; and by
confining himself to these permanent elements, and to the simple character suitable
to the epic style, he may produce and
maintain all the illusion of reality which is

needed to give the full effect to his story.

No doubt a very intimate and accurate acquaintance with the history of the period may be effectual to break the charm—alas! for the hapless wight cursed with a too intrusive knowledge. And it may indeed be that the old historical romances are a delight destined to fade in the noonday glare of science. We shall all eat of the Tree of Knowledge, and shall be as Professors of History knowing fact from fancy. But we shall lose our paradise, and our sorrow shall be greatly multiplied in our conception of the historical novels of the future. In sorrow we shall bring them forth, and we shall read them in the sweat of our brows. I love in my soul, I confess, the 'fearless old fashion' of the old romances: yet the bliss of ignorance cannot perhaps last for ever. Possibly one reason, among others, that we cannot to-day write like Scott and Dumas, is that we are in the fatal transition state between blissful ignorance and complete knowledge. We have not acquired the historical mastery which might enable us, perhaps, to use historical detail naturally and easily; yet we are conscious of the demand for accuracy, and work with the fear of the new broom of historical criticism before our eyes. And in this interval, the hand of the artist is only paralysed by the continual demand of the critic for accuracy, and the yearning of historic science to see the abomination of its own desolation standing also where it ought not, in the temple of Romance.

The foregoing remarks might seem to suggest that it is the romance which charms, and that the historical romance charms not by reason but in spite of its historical character,—the historical character indeed but introducing elements of difficulty and decay. But this is not the case: the charm lies essentially in the historical character. To recognise this, it is enough to let the imagination wander in memory for a few seconds amid the romantic scenes of Scott's historical tales, or the dramatic life of Dumas's great cycles. No, assuredly historical romance has special charms of its own, which the world should not willingly let die.

What a relief it is to get away from ourselves
and our neighbours, our small concerns,
petty jealousies or petty ambitions, and all
the provinciality of our moment of time and
corner of space, to breathe a larger and
more heroic air, at whatever cost of archæo-
logical accuracy: to rub shoulders with
great events, and feel the stir of mighty
principles. And see what boundless wealth
of picturesque character and scenic effect
and dramatic clashings between devotion
to great causes and personal loves and
hates, the field of history offers. Are we
to rob romance of her Paladins, and Hugue-
nots and Covenanters, of her witchcraft,
and her Inquisition, of her Cœur de Lion,
her Richelieu and her Queen of Scots?
What becomes of *Ivanhoe*, without its strife
of English feeling and Norman pride, and
its mediæval Jewbaiting; or of *Les Trois
Mousquetaires* without the political entangle-
ments of loyalty to Richelieu or to the
Queen, which but serve to beat out the
heroic friendships into a nobler harmony?
And more important and valuable to the
story-teller even than this wealth of scenes

and incidents, of great causes and great characters, is the circumambient air of heroism and romance.

Herein we find perhaps the only substitute now left to us for the mystery and magic of the world's wondering youth. Mr. Louis Stevenson has taken the *Arabian Nights* as the crowning type of pure romance. But such tales it is not for us to write upon whom the ends of the world are come. For many of us the haunted and mysterious spaces of unknown history are the next best playing-ground for the imagination, and afford to the romancer the witching gloom or glamour of golden haze, wherewith to work his miracles. So let us still cling to the hope that even under the full blaze of the meridian sun of science, the world will keep apart a shady bower of art where the eyes shall discern artistic excellence in the midst of much inaccuracy, that it may still enjoy Scott's genuine enthusiasm for a possibly misunderstood feudalism, as we enjoy the enthusiasm of the Renaissance for a misunderstood paganism, not merely because in each case the enthusiasm was but the first step to a truer science, but because it was beautiful in itself and produced much beautiful work. However learned the world may grow, it will be an ill day for it when it can no longer take its pleasure in the buoyant narrative and quick invention of Dumas, or in the romantic fancy and healthy humanity of Walter Scott.

THE POET AS HISTORIAN

'Of all Writers under the Sunne, the Poet is the least lier.'
Sir Philip Sidney

THE pretension of the historical novelist
has been very generally challenged. The
right of the poet to treat historical subjects
has, until recently, passed without protest.
Of late, however, as I remarked in discussing
the historical novel, there have not been
wanting signs of a tendency on the part
of historical Science to dispute this right.
Science has exhibited several symptoms of
breaking out in a fresh place. (Mr. Huxley
once called Science a Cinderella. Might not
Bluebeard more fitly serve for a comparison?)
As the first explicit protest that comes to
hand I take a passage from a criticism of
Browning's 'Parleyings,' by a generally acknowledged authority in literary matters.
'We are by no means sure,' wrote the critic,

178

'that poets in creating imaginary characters will in future times continue to think it worth their while to christen them after the characters of history, calling them Thomas à Becket, Mary Stuart, Paracelsus, Sordello, Bernard de Mandeville, and what not. We are by no means sure that they will always consider themselves justified in so doing. As Carlyle has said, the mere facts of history have a special and peculiar preciousness of their own, just because they are facts and not poetic fancies about facts.'

It is rather droll to find Carlyle cited for this high and dry scientific view, Carlyle himself being in the eyes of the sterner sort little better than one of the poets. Professor Seeley, pleading at Birmingham—one would say, a suitable forum—for an organisation of history similar to that by which science was maintained in its seriousness and rigour, in order that history should not any longer live 'under the loose democracy of mere literature,' confounded in a common condemnation Carlyle with Macaulay and other writers of 'delightful history.' The gist of Carlyle's exhortations, moreover, is surely inexcusably perverted. So far from admonishing imaginative writers to confine themselves to their own fictions, Carlyle was for ever expostulating with them for wasting their gifts on unrealities, and urging them to use all the faculties God had given them, to interpret the real men and real deeds that had made the world what it is. 'In the right interpretation of Reality does genuine poetry consist.' This is his express declaration in the essay on Boswell. Homer's *Iliad* he professed he loved precisely because it was not fiction ; nor of Shakespeare was it the fiction that he admired but the fact. 'To say truth, what I most of all admire are the traces he shows of a talent that could have turned the history of England into a kind of *Iliad*, almost perhaps into a kind of Bible.' To *sing* the history of England, that he held would be literature's supremest service.

For Carlyle was well aware of the fundamental truth that history is almost wholly a matter of divination. Our good easy critic talks as if the 'mere facts of history' were to be picked up round and ready, like pebbles on the sea shore. Carlyle knew better. In

a dozen eloquent passages he made lament
that the facts of history had passed into the
impenetrable beyond, that written history
was but matter of inference and interpretation from dubious and perishing clues.
Some of the youngest and most infallible of
our young historical students have sometimes
talked as if they had arrived at the bed-rock
of historical truth, when they had got to the
'original document.' Wiser heads know, alas!
what treacherous sands original documents
may be. It is mighty hard to get at the
'mere facts' of an every day occurrence from
eye-witnesses on oath in a Court of Justice.
Carlyle quotes the old story of Sir Walter
Raleigh looking from his prison windows on
some street tumult, which afterwards three
witnesses reported in three different ways,
himself differing from them all. The merest
facts of history come to us through some
human medium, and come necessarily
coloured by the medium through which they
have passed. Human record, innocent of all
suspicion of ignorance or error or prejudice
or passion, it is idle to look for. The only
question is, whose gloss you will have—the

chronicler's, the state-paper writer's, the
historian's or the poet's. Get away from this
fallible human spirit you cannot. Climb up
into poetry, it is there ; go down to 'scientific'
history, it is there also. 'Mein Freund,' says
Faust to Wagner, eager to plunge into
historical studies and imbue himself with the
spirit of the past,

> die Zeiten der Vergangenheit
> Sind uns ein Buch mit sieben Siegeln.
> Was ihr den Geist der Zeiten heiszt,
> Das ist im Grund der Herren eigner Geist,
> In dem die Zeiten sich bespiegeln.

Yes, for us the past is indeed a book with
seven seals, and the spirit of the past but the
spirit of him that tells the tale. The 'mere
facts of history' in all their special, peculiar
preciousness are simply not to be had.

Let me not be thought guilty for a moment
of the folly of underestimating the importance of documents. Probably the most
characteristic and valuable work of the
century in literature has been to realise the
primary importance of contemporary records,
to explore the 'sources' of history, to discrim-
inate in historical matters what lawyers call
'the best evidence.' Only let us recognise

how short a way the most authentic record
carries us. The most authentic record is
but the narrative of what a man has seen
with his own eyes and heard with his own
ears. How much in the nature of the case
can that be? A word heard here, an act seen
there :—scraps of conversation, isolated deeds,
conjectures of policy, guesses at character.
Real events are complex and simultaneous :
real history moves in the mass. The historian
cannot move a step without comparing, com-
bining, complementing, co-ordinating. The
execution of Mary Queen of Scots, for
example, is a 'mere fact' of history. Well,
the historian cannot begin to tell of it without
a theory of Mary's character, and Elizabeth's,
of the manners and public conscience of the
time, of the aims and motives of the Catholic
powers, of the policy of Elizabeth's ministers
and the temper of her people. Here be
matters beyond documents. The facts of
history while they were not yet history but
actual facts were something singularly different from the valley of dry bones of the
'scientific' historian ; and to breathe through
the bones the breath of life is a matter wholly

beyond the competency of antiquarian research, though organised as seriously and rigorously as Professor Seeley would like to see it. Science has no scales to weigh motives and character, no glass to catch the cross-lights of policy and passion. Nay, the authentic document is dumb, till the historian brings interpretative insight into character to bear on it. 'Alas,' cried Carlyle, the Daniel called to judgment by our scientific critic, 'you read a hundred autograph holograph letters signed Charles Rex with the intensest desire to understand Charles Rex, to know what Charles Rex was and what he had in his eye at that moment : and to no purpose.'

History, then, is necessarily and essentially a work of ideal reconstruction. Is the poet not to be allowed to take a hand in it? Why ! a quickening imagination is the very first thing needful for the attainment of the bare truth. For the most vital part of the historian's task the poet has the most essential qualification. He has the insight into human nature and the quick communion with the purpose of the ages that can read a character from a gesture, a policy from a stray recorded word.

And accordingly we find one of our most
eminent living historians recording his deliberate opinion that for the mere hard purposes
of history the *Iliad* and the *Odyssey* are the
most effective books which ever were written,
and that the most perfect English History
which exists is to be found in the historical
plays of Shakespeare. And here is an interesting fact. Mr. C. H. Firth, who, I suppose,
knows all there is to be known about
Strafford and his times, recently had occasion
to compare the *Life of Strafford*, professedly
by Forster, but now attributed to Robert
Browning, with Browning's tragedy of *Strafford*; and he has pronounced Browning's
poetry to be truer than his history. It was
curious, he said, to contrast the biography
with the play written a year later. In the Life
Browning meant to paint Strafford as he was ;
in the play he painted him as he wished him
to be. And the result is, that with a fuller
knowledge of the records than was possible
for Browning, Mr. Firth finds in several leading incidents the play more adequate than
the Life, and in the whole conception of
Strafford's character the poet nearer to the

truth than the biographer. The intuition of the poet, you see, had rightly amended and supplemented the imperfect records before him.

In the simplest fact or character in history, there is absolutely inexhaustible matter for divination and interpretation. If the world really desire to have the truth of history, it will be wise to discourage neither poet nor plodder, but to encourage workers of the most diverse gifts to present each such aspect thereof as he may have eyes to see or ears to hear. Let the poet utter his vision, and the investigator collate his manuscripts and decipher his inscriptions: and when we have looked upon this picture and that, and fitted the facts into a thousand theories, we may by degrees get some partial insight into the significance of the reality. Experience, Carlyle said, required All-Knowledge to record it.

It cannot, I fear, be denied that poetry has bequeathed to posterity some deluding portraits. But poetry has by no means erred alone. And even here the advantage is with the poet. He does not hold himself out as an historian in the strict sense. There is no rivalry and there should be no deception. Poetry frankly offers itself as imaginative reconstruction, and should mislead no one, whereas the last historian is always for giving us absolute truth. His predecessors may have been ignorant, careless or prejudiced,— too many but palming off a pack of lies upon a credulous world. But with the rising of the latest luminary the mists of error are to scatter, and we are to have 'the pure severity of perfect light.' Happily sagacious readers do not take the historian nearly so seriously as he takes himself. They are perfectly well aware that in his pages they behold not the very men as they lived and breathed, but the best he had wit to piece together from surviving clues. It is Freeman's 'Cnut' or Professor Seeley's Napoleon, every bit as much as it is Browning's Paracelsus or Shakespeare's Hotspur and Harry of Monmouth. The historian, however, tenders his narrative as gospel truth, and the unwary may be misled. No man in his senses can be misled by the Harry and Hotspur that are palpably Shakespeare's Harry and Hotspur and no lesser man's.

If the gallery of historical portraits with

which poetry has enriched the world be not
of a photographic exactitude, they none the
less are 'possessions for ever' more precious
than the great work of Thucydides himself.
If they are not real, they are ideal. Nay,
the mere literary historians, when they err, at
least enrich us with 'delightful history,'
which is a joy for the moment if not a
possession for ever. The scientific historian
does not, I suppose, often fall; but if he falls,
he falls like Lucifer.

What historian is to give us men and women
whom we would take in exchange for Shakespeare's, from Coriolanus to Cleopatra, from
Richard the Second to Queen Katherine?
'Great men,' Mr. Froude has said,—'all *men*
properly so called (whatever is genuine and
natural in them)—lie beyond prose and can
only be really represented by the poet. Whatever may be the cause, the fact is so. Poetry
has this life-giving power and prose has it not;
and thus the poet is the truest historian.'

Or, again, for what amount of information
about the tactics of Agincourt would we
barter such a single line as Henry's?—

'We few, we happy few, we band of brothers.'

Truth? This is truth; this is *the* truth of Agincourt,—the English patriotism, the warrior-kingship, the brotherhood begotten of the common peril. Poetry is truer than the facts. The poets, as Mrs. Browning sang, are

> 'The only truth-tellers now left to God,
> The only speakers of essential truth
> Opposed to relative, comparative
> And temporal truths.'

Poetry, according to the often quoted sentence of Aristotle, is not only nobler but more philosophical than history. Hegel taught that in art were to be found the deepest interests of humanity, the most comprehensive truths of the mind. The truths of poetry he held to be the more genuine reality, the mere facts of experience the crueller deception. About a certain drawing by Prout of a well at Nuremberg, Mr. Ruskin has written : 'All the projecting windows and all the dormers in this square are of wood. But Prout could not stand the inconsistency and deliberately petrified all the wood. Very naughty of him! I have nothing to say in extenuation of this offence ; and

alas! secondly, the houses have, in reality,
only three stories, and he has put a fourth
on, out of his inner consciousness! I never
knew him do such a thing before or since:
but the end of it is, that this drawing of
Nuremberg is immensely more Nurembergy
than the town itself, and a quite glorious
piece of mediæval character.' And if Aristotle and Hegel, and Mrs. Browning and
Mr. Ruskin and Mr. Froude be witnesses
all suspect to the scientific, let me call
Thucydides. Scientific as was his method,
Thucydides too in his famous speeches dared
to be truer than the facts, set himself
avowedly 'to consider principally what might
be pertinently said upon every occasion to
the points in debate.' The actual speakers
of Corcyra or Platæa never, we may be sure,
grasped the import of the situation with the
grip of the great historian; had not the
philosophic insight with which he endows
them. Yet nowhere shall you find truer
Greek history than in those speeches. Poetry
and romance and art distil the spirit of truth
out of the facts. To them we owe the most
vital and fruitful ideas of history. Never in

this work-a-day world was there an historical
Age of Chivalry; never on this sinful earth
an historical Age of Faith. Be sure that
these too are but an 'added gleam,' a 'light
that never was on sea or land,' that here too
we have 'the consecration and the poet's
dream.' The Catholic Church of devout im-
aginations is historically as unreal as Arthur's
Round Table. But in another sense both
Round Table and Church are real with the
highest kind of reality. Such ideals, and
such ideals alone, it is which give any permanent reality to the fleeting generations of
men, who, save in so far as they embody
them in their lives, are but as the beasts that
perish. The real spirit of an age only comes
at last to its proper expression in its secular
poet. Shakespeare is the highest truth of
feudal England, as Dante was the truth of
Catholic Italy or Homer of heroic Greece.
Shakespeare's England is what England had
aspired to be, had striven to be, had attained
to being in certain moments and in certain
men :

'This royal throne of kings, this sceptred isle,
  This earth of majesty, this seat of Mars,

This other Eden, demi-paradise,
This fortress built by Nature for herself
Against infection and the hand of war,
This happy breed of men, this little world,
This precious stone set in the silver sea,
Which serves it in the office of a wall,
Or as a moat defensive to a house,
Against the envy of less happier lands,
This blessed plot, this earth, this realm, this England.'

All honour then to the scientific investigator; but honour likewise to the 'delightful-historians,' and glory in the highest to Shakespeare and the poets. For, as Wordsworth finely said: ' Poetry is the breath and finer spirit of all knowledge; it is the impassioned expression which is in the countenance of all Science. Poetry is the first and last of all knowledge—it is as immortal as the heart of man.'

THE GREAT WORK

A WRITER in the *Daily News*, for reasons of his own, entered a protest lately against what he called the *Magnum Opus* theory. A man's friends and acquaintance, he complained, were continually urging him to write a Great Work. It was in vain that the victim protested that he did not want to write a Great Work; or that he had written a Great Work which nobody ever heard of; or that he could not live (in this mortal state) by a Great Work, and must produce things which would yield him his daily bread. He might have added that if he did write one, the very last to read it would be these same monitors.

That a man's female relations should hug the delusion that he was born for some high emprise and should persist in exhortation is, no doubt, in the order of nature. But

less prejudiced advisers should know better.
Certainly censors, whose admonitions get
uttered in print, should know better. Believe
me, the man who has a Great Work in him
does not, save in very exceptional cases, require to have the sides of his intent pricked
by the casual friend or the indolent irresponsible reviewer. Once in a way, a George
Eliot may wait for the encouragement of a
George Henry Lewes to turn from West-
minster Reviewing to *Scenes of Clerical Life.*
But in ninety-nine cases out of a hundred it
is true that, admonition or no admonition, a
man does exactly what he has it in him to
do. If a man is not a Balzac, it is in vain
that you will urge him to write a *Comédie
Humaine.* If on the other hand he has a
Comédie Humaine in him, he will go on writing rubbish for ten years, in the teeth of
parental remonstrance and public neglect,
sustained by inward consciousness of power
in the sure and certain hope that some
day he will produce the Great Work and
be famous.

From gentlemen with a bent for admonition, it must be said parenthetically, there is

absolutely no way of escape. Delight your
generation with occasional verse or graceful
essays full of scholarship and urbane wit, and
you are sternly bidden, or perhaps urged by
way of flattering expostulation, to leave such
trifling and do something worthy of your
abilities. Essay an epic, and you are recommended to content yourself with shorter
flights. The three-volume novelist is reminded that bigness is not greatness. Masters
of the short story are exhorted to do something more 'important.' One man pleads
modestly, that to earn his living he must
defer to the popular taste, and it is hinted
that he is selling his birthright for a mess of
pottage. Another in the proud consciousness of genius scorns to prostitute his Muse,
and he is soundly rated for not thinking
first of his family and his social obligations.
You lead a life of literary leisure like
Edward Fitzgerald, and you are reproved
for giving the time to writing letters to
your friends which ought to have been
given to writing books for the publishers.
You throw your soul into poetry like
Shelley's, or novels like George Sand's, and

in the end the Olympian critic serenely
pronounces that nothing but your private
letters will live.

But about this *Magnum Opus*. There have
been men no doubt, men of genius, who have
said to themselves deliberately, 'Go to, I will
write a Great Work.' For example, there
was Gibbon. Everybody remembers the passage where Gibbon tells how the idea of his
History occurred to him. 'It was at Rome
on the 15th of October 1764, as I sat musing
amidst the ruins of the Capitol, while the
bare-footed friars were singing vespers in the
temple of Jupiter, that the idea of writing
the decline and fall of the city first started to
my mind.' And everybody knows to what
good purpose he devoted himself to carrying
out the conception into superb accomplishment. But for our present purpose, the interesting thing about Gibbon's case is, that
he had made up his extremely well-regulated
mind to write a great work of some sort, long
before he had a glimmering of what the great
work was to be. Then with equal delibera-
tion he set about choosing a subject. Already
in 1761, then at the age of twenty-five, he

had passed in review a number of subjects
for a large historical composition, and had at
length selected the expedition of Charles VIII.
of France into Italy. After this he succes-
sively chose and rejected the Crusade of
Richard Cœur de Lion, the Barons' Wars
against John and Henry III., the history of
Edward the Black Prince, the lives and com-
parisons of Henry V. and the Emperor Titus,
the life of Sir Philip Sidney, and the life of
the Marquis of Montrose. At length he
seemed to have fixed on Sir Walter Raleigh
for his hero ; he was attracted by his eventful
story, varied by the characters of the soldier
and the sailor, the courtier and the historian.
Romantic subjects all of them, and so far
not a hint of predilection for the period and
subject which were to make him immortal.
The next choice was equally wide of his
final mark, the history namely of the Liberty
of the Swiss, of that independence which a
brave people rescued from the House of
Austria, defended against a Dauphin of
France, and finally sealed. From such a
theme, so full of public spirit, of military
glory, of examples of virtue, of lessons of

government, the dullest stranger would catch
fire. What might not himself hope, whose
talents, whatsoever they might be, would be
influenced with the zeal of partiotism? For
Switzerland was Gibbon's fatherland by adop-
tion; it was the true *alma mater* to one who
found the breasts of Oxford dry; and, finally,
it was the country of Mlle. Curchod, the
heroine and victim of the famous love-story
in one sentence of the iconoclastic historian,
'who sighed as a lover and obeyed as a son.'
This subject was rejected because the sources
were inaccessible, fast locked in the obscurity
of an old barbarous German dialect, which
he was ignorant of and not disposed to grapple
with. By way of contrast he had in his mind's
eye a history of the Republic of Florence,
under the House of the Medici;—singular
men and singular events, the Medicis four
times expelled and as often recalled, and the
Genius of Freedom reluctantly yielding to
the army of Charles v.; the character and
fate of Savonarola, and the revival of arts
and letters in Italy. At this point, in his
search for subjects, came his foreign tour and
the sojourn in Rome, during which, as we

have seen, his true subject was revealed to him in a flash.

I have dwelt on Gibbon's case, partly to show the kind of mind which may dream of great works without imputation of fatuity ; partly to show my own candour. Because it undoubtedly is a genuine case to support the theory of the *Magnum Opus*. Here was a youth with no notion what the work was to be, but possessed with a fixed idea that it was to be a Great Work. And the *Decline and Fall of the Roman Empire* is a great work ; of that there can be no possible shadow of doubt.

Then, again, there is Bacon. There is a tradition that at sixteen, or thereabouts, young Francis Bacon had already determined to revolutionise the whole frame of human thought. That is no uncommon determination to come to at the age of sixteen. What is less common is that at sixty people should be able to persuade even themselves that they have done it. Least common of all is it for them to be able to persuade anybody else of that. Whether the story of Bacon be true or apocryphal, at any rate at the age of thirty-one, which is not old as we count oldness now, he wrote to his uncle, Lord Burleigh, calmly informing him that he had taken all knowledge to be his province. How Lord Burleigh must have nodded! Yet in due course there did veritably come the *Instauratio Magna*, the greatest birth of time!

Or to come to our own less spacious times, consider the magnificence of fixed resolve with which Mr. Herbert Spencer announced already in a prospectus of 1860 the whole mighty scheme of his System of Philosophy. It was to be gradually unfolded in five great treatises, each with its contents already mapped out under multitudinous headings and sub-headings. With unhasting, unresting persistency he has kept labouring at his monstrous programme ever since! One of the reasons he gave for printing that prospectus was, that the outline of the scheme should remain, in case he should not live to complete the system. There you have the true spirit of the devotee of the *Magnum Opus*.

One needs be very sure of one's-self, and sure of a steady independent income to boot,

even with genius, to deliberately embark on
a Great Work. Gibbon was singularly sure
of himself and enjoyed a monetary competency. Bacon was equally sure of himself,
and got money independently of his philosophy in one way or the other, especially, it
has been said, the other. The worst of it is
that a man may be as sure of himself as
Gibbon or Bacon, and after all produce
instead of a *Decline and Fall of the Roman
Empire* or a *Novum Organum*, an abortive
Key to All Mythologies or a monumental
History of Europe to prove that Providence
is on the side of the Tories.

The late Mr. Buckle sacrificed his health to
his historical labours. He travelled abroad
to regain strength for more work, caught a
fever at Damascus and died. Almost his
last conscious words were 'My book, my
book! I shall never finish my book!' Is it
not pathetic to think of?

Providence, whether or not it is always on
the side of the big battalions, is by no means
always on the side of the big books. It is
a solemn thing to sacrifice one's life, the
only life of the sort one has, in manufactur-

ing a book like Alison's History of Europe,
only to fill with its voluminous respectability
an undisturbed shelf in every second-hand
bookshop in the kingdom. Really, upon a
rational calculation of the chances, it seems
wiser for a young man just to rejoice in his
youth, than to use it up in preparing or projecting a monumental History or a System
of Synthetic Philosophy or a Key to all the
Mythologies, for all which things too, remember, God will bring him to judgment.

Well, perhaps, if we are to have world-
histories and philosophic systems, the risk
must be faced. It may be as in love so in
literature,

> ' He either fears his fate too much,
>   Or his deserts are small,
> Who dares not put it to the touch
>   To gain or lose it all.'

It was in truth a gallant sight to see Freeman at his age, and alas! with enfeebled
health, attacking on so lordly a scale so large
a subject as the History of Sicily. It had
been his first historical love ; the Rosaline to
the Juliet he wedded first after all, that
finely-developed Juliet, *The Norman Con-*

quest. More than once he dwelt lovingly on the supreme interest and importance throughout history (he would not let us talk of ancient and modern history), of this mid-Mediterranean island, this old battlefield of decisive race-struggles. And when Juliet was on the shelf, he turned once more to woo Rosaline. The first two volumes on the magnificent scale of the Clarendon Press brought that history only to the eve of the struggle in the Peloponnesian War. Let the clever young man who dashes off his essay or his epigram between tea and dinner, pause to consider the nature of the task Freeman was undertaking and take off his hat to this dauntless spirit. Nay, let him take off his hat, not to the veteran leader only, but—for research is a thing needful—to the rank and file, whether they are marching to the glory of Gibbon or the grave of Alison. The body of the most muddleheaded may fill a trench over which some day an historian of genius may pass to victory.

And yet, and yet the irresponsible young man is sometimes tempted to hint that to-day it is not so much the *magnum* as the *maximum opus* that our industrious workers seem bent upon producing. Macaulay's historical essays, some learned men say, are wofully inaccurate. So conscious was Macaulay himself of the imperfection of his essays that he pleaded that his hand had been forced by unauthorised American publication or he would never have republished them. Yet these essays are at least as full of life as ever, while many an historical *Magnum Opus* is stone-dead. One ventures to hope and believe that when the novelty of laying open valuable historical sources has passed, when the mass of new material has been not only displayed but digested, the historian, without sacrifice of science, will once more have some conscience for form. Great histories, great beyond all cavilling, have been written, which can be comfortably packed into a Tauchnitz pocket-volume or two.

When Victor Cousin, willing like Hercules —as Heine cruelly remarked—to wear the lion's skin as well as to ply the distaff, asked Hegel for a succinct account of his system, he got severely snubbed. These things, the German philosopher drily replied, were not to be said succinctly, particularly in French. Yet the longest of the Platonic dialogues is not longer than a shilling story book ; and Descartes's Discourse can be read almost at a sitting. And if Hegel himself and Aristotle bulk large, it should be borne in mind that most of the volumes are but made up from notes of lectures.

The literary temper dislikes and distrusts bulk and big pretensions, abhors system-mongering. Montaigne could not away with 'Cicero's prefaces, definitions, divisions, which surcharged and confounded with long and far-fetched preambles whatsoever quick, wittie and pithie conceit was in him.' Those logical and Aristotelian ordinances were not, he said, 'availfull' for him. He loved like Bacon to 'toss' his thought. This phrase of Bacon greatly took Edward Fitzgerald's fancy, likewise a typical specimen of the literary temper. So Matthew Arnold gibed at the 'system of philosophy with principles coherent, independent, subordinate and derivative' of Mr. Frederic Harrison's 'French pedant.' So Mr. Pater has lately protested he cannot help hearing the rattle of the dry bones in the dogmatic systems of Aristotle, Aquinas, and Spinoza. 'Distinguished German philosophers,' wrote Heine, 'who may accidently cast a glance over these pages'— the pages in question were his *Religion and Philosophy in Germany*, Heine's attempt to expound to Frenchmen what the German philosophers were driving at—'will superciliously shrug their shoulders at the meagreness and incompleteness of all which I here offer. But they will be kind enough to bear in mind that the little which I say is expressed clearly and intelligibly, whereas their own works, although very profound—unfathomably profound—very deep—stupendously, deep—are in the same degree unintelligible. Of what benefit to the people is the grain locked away in great granaries, to which they have no key? The masses are famishing for knowledge, and will thank me for the portion of intellectual bread, small though it be, which I honestly share with them . . . I am not one of the seven hundred wise men of Germany. I stand with the great masses at the portals of their wisdom. And if a truth slips through, and if this truth falls in my way,

then I write it with pretty letters on paper,
and give it to the compositor, who sets it in
leaden type and gives it to the printer ; the
printer prints it, and then it belongs to the
whole world.'

Even in the case of so English a philosopher
as Lord Bacon, we remember that James I.
who, if a fool, was at least acknowledged to
be the wisest fool in Christendom, compared
the *Novum Organum* to the peace which
passeth understanding. Not James nor anybody else, wise or foolish, ever said anything
of that kind about the *Essays*, those wonderful short *Essays*. As Bacon said of them in
his own day, so have they been ever since,
' of all his other works, the most current, for
that it seems, they come home to men's
business and bosoms.'

It is not, however, in the sphere of philosophy or history or science, but in the sphere
of literature proper, that the theory of the
Magnum Opus and the exhortations and
protests founded thereon are so absurd, fly
so directly, as it seems to me, in the face of
the facts of literary history. With one or
two rare and remarkable exceptions, it has

not been by saying, 'Go to, we will write a *Magnum Opus*,' that in this sphere the most enduring books have been written. Flaubert—and I give the adherents of the theory I deprecate the full benefit of his name as I pass—Flaubert marvelled that Sainte-Beuve should be content to go on writing for the newspapers, when he was not in want of food and might write books. Yet books, big books, have been written, and printed too, of less enduring value than the *Causeries*. Heine just wrote off a description of a walking-tour, and the *Reisebilder* are immortal. In writing *The Compleat Angler*, Walton said he did but make 'a recreation of a recreation.' Addison and Steele wrote papers to amuse the town, and Sir Roger de Coverley has outlived Cato. Mat Prior has considerably more life in him than Robert Montgomery, the efficient elixir of Macaulay notwithstanding; and it is not by his *Solomon, a Poem in Three Books*, that Mat Prior lives. Montaigne carries his years at least as well as Montesquieu. And certain stray papers written out of office-hours for a magazine by a clerk of the India House have outlived the more ambitious works of two

other distinguished servants of John Company, the Mills, father and son, with their
Analyses of the Phenomena of the Human
Mind and their Systems of Logic Ratiocina-
tive and Inductive.

What could be more unpremeditated than
the way in which that almost nameless throng
of singers poured forth their songs, who made
of Elizabethan England a nest of singing
birds? In those brave days their fashion
was to throw off, or affect to throw off, their
tuneful trifles without a thought of publication. For publication they meditated, or
affected to meditate, some *Magnum Opus* to
come later to justify them. But they would
show these trifles to their friends ; and these
friends would persuade them to publish, or,
bold bad men, would take the bull by the
horns and send the poems to the printer
themselves.

'Courteous reader,' writes W. Percy by way
of preface to his Cycle of Sonnets to the Fairest
Cælia, 'whereas I was fully determined to
have concealed my Sonnets as things privy
to myself, yet, of courtesy having lent them
to some they were secretly committed to the

Press and almost finished before it came to
my knowledge. Wherefore, making as they
say, Virtue of Necessity, I did deem it most
convenient to propose my epistle, only to
beseech you to account of them as of toys
and amorous devices; and ere long, I will
impart unto the World another Poem, which
shall be both more fruitful and ponderous.
In the meanwhile I commit these as a
pledge to your indifferent censure. W. Percy.
London 1594.' You see the indiscreet friend
served the bashful Elizabethan the same turn
that the American pirate served the bashful
Macaulay. These Elizabethan toys and
amorous devices are as fresh to-day as three
centuries ago, and thanks to Dr. Grosart, Mr.
Arber, and Mr. Arthur Bullen, are still
ministering to our exceeding great enjoy-
ment. Whether W. Percy ever imparted to
the world his more fruitful and ponderous
poem I am not Elizabethan scholar enough
to say. At least I never heard of it. If he
did, I dare swear it is not without reasons
that the Sonnets to Cælia, which are not by
any means the happiest example of Elizabethan sonneteering, are still afloat, while

the ponderous poem has gone to the
bottom.

Lest such promises of a *Magnum Opus* to
follow should be accounted the mere cox-
combry of conventional mock-modesty, let
me remind you, that in just such wise did
Prior excuse himself for dedicating his light
occasional verse to his Mæcenas Lord Dor-
set. 'I humbly hope that as I may hereafter
bind up my fuller sheaf and lay some pieces
of a very different Nature (the product of
my severer Studies) at your Lordship's Feet,
I shall engage your more serious reflection,' etc. Now Prior kept this promise. He
achieved his *Magnum Opus*, the product of
his severer studies, a piece of a very different
nature from *Paulo Purganti* and *Hans Carvel.*
It was *Solomon, a Poem in Three Books.* We
hope it engaged his lordship's more serious
reflections. At least it seems worthy to
engage our serious reflection in connection
with the present discussion.

Pass to the supreme name not only in
Elizabethan but in all literature. Shakespeare simply did with all his might the
theatrical work which came to his hand.

Glorious as the work is, it was work done as
a hack-playwright. All the little evidence
we have points to that, all except Mr.
Donnelly's: his position at the theatre; the
sneers of the University wits; the traces of
his manner of work, first his furbishing up
of stock pieces, then his gradually transform-
ing them by his genius, as occasion offered
and as he felt his genius firm under him;
and finally, for crowning proof, his placid
early retirement, leaving a body of actors to
complete the famous first folio without his
assistance or direction. Not, mind you, that
Shakespeare was not keenly and fully alive
to the omnipotence of his genius; you have
but to turn to the Sonnets to recognise serene
pride of genius and a sense of triumphant
achievement. But the set production of
Magna Opera was, it would seem, the very
last of his thoughts.

Certainly it was the very last of Scott's
thoughts, when he poured forth the *Waverley
Novels* in anonymous profusion. The famous
collected edition of the novels is always
referred to in Scott's *Journal* as the *Opus
Magnum*; but if ever there was a man free

from all tinge of the superstition of the
Magnum Opus that man was Walter Scott.
Unless we had the convincing evidence of
Lockhart's book and Scott's own letters and
prefaces to prove it, it would be unimaginable
that this Wizard of Romance should have
flung forth his wonders with so unpremeditated prodigality and held by them and
the fame of them so lightly. To remember
the frank, unaffected, manly modesty of this
man, who justly enjoyed in his lifetime
unrivalled literary prestige ; to think of the
nonchalance of this giant, of the simplicity of
spirit in which he poured out his immortal
tales ; and then to think of the punctilios
and pretensions and professions and protesta-
tions of the novelists of the hour is matter
for tears and laughter.

Scott with characteristic modesty had con-
sulted James Ballantyne as to his hopes of
him as a novelist. James's hopes were not
high. Scott saw it at a glance ; but all he
said was that he did not see why he should
not succeed as well as other people,—that is,
remember, as well as 'Monk' Lewis and
Mrs. Radcliffe and Jane Porter. 'The

Edinbro' faith now is,' wrote Scott to Mr.
Morritt, one of the very few to whom from
the first he entrusted the secret of the authorship, 'that *Waverley* is written by Jeffrey,
having been composed to lighten the tedium
of his late Transatlantic voyage. So you see
the unknown infant is like to come to prefer-
ment. In truth I am not sure it would be
considered quite decorous for me, as a Clerk of
Session, to write novels. Judges being monks,
clerks are a sort of lay brethren from whom
some solemnity of walk and conduct may be
expected. So whatever I may do of this
kind, I shall whistle down the wind to prey on
fortune.' And the preface to the third edition
of *Waverley* was in just the same strain of
unaffected modesty. And if this was before
the new success or in the early days of it,
you may see how lasting his mood was by
reading the prefaces in the collected edition
of 1829-30, long after his literary empire, all
unsolicited, had been universally acknowledged. Read, for example, the preface to
Ivanhoe, the novel which had been received
with a perfect acclaim of applause. Never
was there less blowing of the trumpet in

the new moon to accompany the birth of masterpieces. Scott was simply filled full to the lips with romance, and when his hour came he just let himself go. You remember the anecdote in Lockhart, of the hand ceaselessly writing which so bothered Menzies in his cups? 'I have been watching it,—it fascinates my eye—it never stops,—page after page is finished and thrown on a heap of MS., and still it goes on unwearied; and so it will be till candles are brought in, and God knows how long after that. It is the same every night,—I can't stand the sight of it, when I am not at my books.' 'Some stupid, dogged, engrossing clerk, probably,' exclaimed some giddy youth in the company. 'No, boys,' answered their host; 'I well know what hand it is—'tis Walter Scott's.' And when it came to still more rapid dictation, Scott preferred John Ballantyne as an amanuensis to Willie Laidlaw, because his pen was the faster and also because he kept it to the paper without interruption, though with many an arch twinkle in his eyes and now and then an audible smack of his lips. Whereas Laidlaw entered with such keen

zest into the interest of the story as it flowed
from the author's lips, that he could not
forbear interrupting with his, 'Gude keep us
a'! the like o' that—eh, sirs, eh, sirs!' Thus
was composed no less a work than the *Bride
of Lammermoor* in the midst of intense
physical suffering, the affectionate Laidlaw
beseeching Scott to stop dictating, when his
audible suffering filled every pause. 'Nay,
Willie,' was the answer, 'only see the doors
are fast. I would fain keep all the cry as
well as all the wool to ourselves.'

While we are among these kingly names,
let me be candid and make a present of one
to the enemy. For one, and one of the
mightiest, of the lords of English poetic
literature the set production of a *Magnum
Opus* was the first and the last thought.
Milton's was a life dedicated from the
beginning. By the age of twenty-three, as
appears from a letter to a Cambridge friend
enclosing the second sonnet, he was
cherishing a long formed resolve to devote
his life to some great work. This was his
apology for standing aloof from the ordinary
money-getting pursuits of early manhood.

This was his excuse for his late spring,
which still no bud nor blossom showed, as
the sonnet phrased it. With this aspiration
he encouraged himself, when he became
'something suspicious of himself and did
take notice of a certain belatedness in him.'
His deliberate aim was self-cultivation and
self-devotion to the accomplishment of some
great thing. Very early he found and took
poetry to be his vocation. At twenty-eight
he wrote the famous letter to his friend
Diodati. 'What am I thinking of? Why,
with God's help, of immortality! Forgive
the word, I only whisper it in your ear!
Yes, I am pluming my wings for a flight.'
He wrote so at the end of the Horton
period, when the minor poems had already
been given to the world, and he had already
done enough, you might have thought, for
one life's fame. The following year we find
him casting his thoughts, as so many of our
greatest poets have done, on the legend of
Arthur for the subject of his great poem.
Then in 1641, being thirty-two years of age,
he publicly uttered his *apologia* and confessed his aspirations.

'None hath by more studious ways endeavoured, and with more unwearied spirit
none shall—that I dare almost aver of
myself, as far as life and full licence will
extend. Neither do I think it shame to
covenant with any knowing reader that for
some few years yet I may go on trust with
him toward the payment of what I am now
indebted, as being a work not to be raised
from the heat of youth, or the vapours of
wine, like that which flows at waste from
the pen of some vulgar amorist, or the
trencher fury of a rhyming parasite, nor to
be obtained by the invocation of Dame
Memory and her siren daughters, but by
devout prayer to that Eternal Spirit, who
can enrich with all utterance and knowledge, and sends out his seraphim with the
hallowed fire of his altar to touch and
purify the life of whom he pleases. To this
must be added industrious, select reading,
steady observation, insight into all seemly
and generous acts and affairs. Till
which in some measure be compassed, at
mine own peril and cost, I refuse not to
sustain this expectation, from as many as

are not loth to hazard so much credulity
upon the best pledges that I can give them.'

And again in that famous and often
quoted passage:

'Perceiving that some trifles which I had
in memory, composed at under twenty or
thereabouts, met with acceptance . . . I
began to assent to them (my Italian friends)
and divers of my friends here at home, and
not less to an inward prompting, which
now grows daily upon me, that by labour
and intent study, which I take to be my
portion in this life, joined with the strong
propensity of nature, I might perhaps leave
something so written to aftertimes as they
should not willingly let it die.'

And the accomplishment of this noble
vow, the end of this nobly dedicated life,
was the sublime Puritan Epic, *Paradise Lost*.

There, I hope that I have given away a
handsome enough present in Milton. Yet
really I am making no concession at all.
Milton did say to himself, 'Go to, I will
write a Great Work,' but therein he only
followed 'the strong propensity of nature.'
He did precisely what he had it in him to

do. He, if ever any man, had the call from within. Such call when vouchsafed let all men follow. All my protest is against the call from without. Conceive, if you can, Milton turned aside from his high and almost holy purpose by the allurements of journalism or the needs of the passing hour. Why, a civil war failed to turn him aside, and, a closer affliction still, his own total blindness. Neither the Protectorate and political employment, nor the Restoration and political disgrace, could make him forget his call. It is a flattering but mistaken and misleading notion, that the gentlemen who do political squibs and literary *causerie* for the newspapers could, by simply taking thought, add several thousand cubits to their stature and write a *Paradise Lost.* Take, by the way of example, the man who has sometimes been regarded, who regarded himself, as a victim sacrificed to journalistic task-work, the man whose life suggested the remarks in the *Daily News* with which I started, Théophile Gautier. What are the odds, if Gautier had been free from the obligation to turn out a weekly dramatic *feuilleton*, that he would have given the world any better poetry than *Emaux et Camées*? Are not the chances rather that, without the pressure of daily needs, we should have had to go without many of the very delightful volumes we now have from his pen, and have got nothing whatever in their place? Anyway, the story goes, and it is an odd story when you come to think of it, that the young Théo in early manhood had to be shut up in his bedroom by his mother, to write *Mademoiselle de Maupin*!

Some bold spirits have not feared even in Milton's own case to take their stand against the superstition of the *Magnum Opus*. They would that he had dwelt all his life amid the glades of Horton and gone on giving them the magic of the minor poems. They lament the sacrifice of the poet of *Comus* and *Lycidas* to the poet of the *Paradise Lost*. They regret that many priceless trinkets and much matchless filigree work, which would have lent adornment and pleasantness to their daily living, must have been melted down to make that cold colossal statue. It is a fact at least, no doubt, that

dozens have *Lycidas* by heart, for every
reader who gets beyond the first book of
the great Epic. The readers indeed of the
twelve books of *Paradise Lost* are probably
as select a band as the readers of the twelve
cantos of the *Faerie Queene*, another of the
Magna Opera of our poetic literature.
Edgar Poe, who of course dearly loved a
paradox, and who had besides a theory of
his own about poetry to support, went so far
as to maintain that *Paradise Lost* was only
to be enjoyed by being regarded as a series
of minor poems!

Finally, let not the advocates of the
Magnum Opus pretend that, at worst, these
admonitions of theirs have a bracing effect
and can do no harm. They may do a great
deal of harm. There are instances to cite
where the harm has been done. If Milton
is the saint of the true religion of the *Magnum Opus*, the superstition does not want
for martyrs. If I am not mistaken, the
late Mr. Cotter Morison was a man of great
ability sterilised by too high ideals. Mark
Pattison was another martyr to the theory.
Not content to put forth just what he had

to put forth, he was ever gathering, pruning, preparing for something big to come—which never came. The result was that his temper seemed to have been soured, his life was largely a wasted life, and the world never reaped adequate advantage from his unquestioned ability and erudition.

Mark Pattison made Isaac Casaubon a text for a sermon on the creed of the *Magnum Opus*, and for a denunciation of the modern world of letters that knew nothing of the self-denial, the unremitting effort, the incessant mental tension, the devotion of a life, which was the scholar's portion. But is not Casaubon, like Pattison, a warning rather than encouraging example of the theory? What I say of Pattison. Pattison has to admit of Casaubon—his *Magnum Opus* never came after all. It was put off and put off for more reading and ever more reading and note-taking. The excuse is a lofty ideal and the interruptions of the world. Casaubon's Diary like Pattison's *Memoirs* is full of moaning and groaning over the shortness of the time and the obstacles to study. But Pattison confesses that Casaubon had (as he himself had) as much leisure as is possible to mortal man. He confesses that for Casaubon's aims, no amount of leisure would have sufficed. It is a *reductio ad absurdum* of his theory. And one cannot avoid a suspicion that these too lofty ideals are apt to be but a cloak for a highly respectable species of mental indolence, the flattering unction laid to the secretly dissatisfied soul. Both Casaubon and Pattison, one shrewdly suspects, liked reading and disliked writing. They went on accumulating notes to postpone the painful effort necessary to set their accumulated materials in order and to build therewith the great work itself. This is not mental tension, but mental indolence. The faults of Will Ladislaw and Mr. Casaubon in *Middlemarch* were more akin than they suspected.

If Mr. Casaubon in *Middlemarch* had contented himself with something short of a Key to all Mythologies, had contributed, let us say, pithy paragraphs to *The Guardian*, he would have been a more profitable writer as well as a better husband.

The typical martyr was the unhappy Amiel. Had not his friends insisted upon his regarding himself as a genius, he might have lived a prosperous life as a Swiss gentleman and father of a family, doing his duty in that state of life in which it had pleased God to call him as a lecturer to ladies. But once he got into his head that he was a genius from whom great things were expected, his life thenceforth was the life of the impotent man, longing, yet powerless, to struggle down into the troubled waters of literary production into which others continually plunged before his eyes. So he maundered in a *Journal Intime*. When people talk of the slavery of journalism, at least let it be confessed that it is better to be the slave of any respectable public journal than the slave of a *Journal Intime*.

Printed by T. and A. CONSTABLE, Printers to Her Majesty,
at the Edinburgh University Press.

List of Books

in

Belles Lettres

Elkin Mathews
& John Lane:
Publishers
and Vendors of
Choice & Rare
Editions in
Belles Lettres.

ALL BOOKS IN THIS CATALOGUE
ARE PUBLISHED AT NET PRICES

1894

Telegraphic Address—
'BODLEIAN, LONDON'

A WORD must be said for the manner in which the publishers have produced the volume (*i.e.* "The Earth Fiend"), a sumptuous folio, printed by CONSTABLE, the etchings on Japanese paper by MR. GOULDING. The volume should add not only to MR. STRANG'S fame but to that of MESSRS. ELKIN MATHEWS AND JOHN LANE, who are rapidly gaining distinction for their beautiful editions of belles-lettres.'—*Daily Chronicle*, Sept. 24, 1892.

Referring to MR. LE GALLIENNE'S 'English Poems' *and* 'Silhouettes' by MR. ARTHUR SYMONS :—' We only refer to them now to note a fact which they illustrate, and which we have been observing of late, namely, the recovery to a certain extent of good taste in the matter of printing and binding books. These two books, which are turned out by MESSRS. ELKIN MATHEWS AND JOHN LANE, are models of artistic publishing, and yet they are simplicity itself. The books with their excellent printing and their very simplicity make a harmony which is satisfying to the artistic sense.'—*Sunday Sun*, Oct. 2, 1892.

'MR. LE GALLIENNE is a fortunate young gentleman. I don't know by what legerdemain he and his publishers work, but here, in an age as stony to poetry as the ages of Chatterton and Richard Savage, we find the full edition of his book sold before publication. How is it done, MESSRS. ELKIN MATHEWS AND JOHN LANE? for, without depreciating MR. LE GALLIENNE'S sweetness and charm, I doubt that the marvel would have been wrought under another publisher. These publishers, indeed, produce books so delightfully that it must give an added pleasure to the hoarding of first editions.'—KATHARINE TYNAN in *The Irish Daily Independent*.

'To MESSRS. ELKIN MATHEWS AND JOHN LANE almost more than to any other, we take it, are the thanks of the grateful singer especially due ; for it is they who have managed, by means of limited editions and charming workmanship, to impress book-buyers with the belief that a volume may have an æsthetic and commercial value. They have made it possible to speculate in the latest discovered poet, as in a new company—with the difference that an operation in the former can be done with three half-crowns.'

St. James's Gazette.

List of Books

IN

BELLES LETTRES

(*Including some Transfers*)

PUBLISHED BY

Elkin Mathews and John Lane

The Bodley Head

VIGO STREET, LONDON, W.

N.B.—The Authors and Publishers reserve the right of reprinting any book in this list if a second edition is called for, except in cases where a stipulation has been made to the contrary, and of printing a separate edition of any of the books for America irrespective of the numbers to which the English editions are limited. The numbers mentioned do not include the copies sent for review or to the public libraries.

———◆———

ADAMS (FRANCIS).
  ESSAYS IN MODERNITY. Cr. 8vo. 5s. net. [*In preparation.*]
ALLEN (GRANT).
  THE LOWER SLOPES: A Volume of Verse. 600 copies.
  Cr. 8vo. 5s. net. [*Immediately.*]
ANTÆUS.
  THE BACKSLIDER AND OTHER POEMS. 100 only.
  Small 4to. 7s. 6d. net. [*Very few remain.*]
BEECHING (H. C.), J. W. MACKAIL, &
  J. B. B. NICHOLS.
  LOVE IN IDLENESS. With Vignette by W. B. SCOTT.
  Fcap. 8vo, half vellum. 12s. net. [*Very few remain.*]
  Transferred by the Authors to the present Publishers.

BENSON (ARTHUR CHRISTOPHER).
POEMS.   550 copies.   Fcap. 8vo.   5s. net.
[*Very few remain.*

BENSON (EUGENE).
FROM THE ASOLAN HILLS : A Poem.   300 copies.   Imp.
16mo.   5s. net.   [*Very few remain.*

BINYON (LAURENCE).
POEMS.   16mo.   5s. net.   [*In preparation.*

BOURDILLON (F. W.).
A LOST GOD : A Poem.   With Illustrations by H. J. FORD.
500 copies.   8vo.   6s. net.   [*Very few remain.*

BOURDILLON (F. W.).
AILES D'ALOUETTE.   Poems printed at the private press
of Rev. H. DANIEL, Oxford.   100 only.   16mo.
£1, 10s. net.   [*Not published.*

BRIDGES (ROBERT).
THE GROWTH OF LOVE.   Printed in Fell's old English
type at the private press of Rev. H. DANIEL, Oxford.
100 only.   Fcap. 4to.   £2, 12s. 6d. net.
[*Not published.*

COLERIDGE (HON. STEPHEN).
THE SANCTITY OF CONFESSION : A Romance.   Second
Edition.   Crown 8vo.   3s. net.   [*A few remain.*

CRANE (WALTER).
RENASCENCE : A Book of Verse.   Frontispiece and 38
designs by the Author.
[*Small paper edition out of print.*
There remain a few large paper copies, fcap. 4to.   £1, 1s. net.
And a few fcap. 4to, Japanese vellum.   £1, 15s. net.

CROSSING (WM.).
THE ANCIENT CROSSES OF DARTMOOR.   With 11 plates.
8vo, cloth.   4s. 6d. net.   [*Very few remain.*

DAVIDSON (JOHN).

PLAYS: An Unhistorical Pastoral; A Romantic Farce; Bruce, a Chronicle Play; Smith, a Tragic Farce; Scaramouch in Naxos, a Pantomime, with a Frontispiece, Title-page, and Cover Design by AUBREY BEARDSLEY. 500 copies. Small 4to. 7s. 6d. net.
[Immediately.

DAVIDSON (JOHN).

FLEET STREET ECLOGUES. Second Edition. Fcap. 8vo, buckram. 5s. net.

DAVIDSON (JOHN).

A RANDOM ITINERARY: Prose Sketches, with a Ballad. Frontispiece, Title-page, and Cover Design by LAURENCE HOUSMAN. Fcap. 8vo. Uniform with 'Fleet Street Eclogues.' 5s. net.

DAVIDSON (JOHN).

THE NORTH WALL. Fcap. 8vo. 2s. 6d. net.
The few remaining copies transferred by the Author to the present Publishers.

DE GRUCHY (AUGUSTA).

UNDER THE HAWTHORN, AND OTHER VERSES. Frontispiece by WALTER CRANE. 300 copies. Crown 8vo. 5s. net. *[Very few remain.*
Also 30 copies on Japanese vellum. 15s. net.

DE TABLEY (LORD).

POEMS, DRAMATIC AND LYRICAL. By JOHN LEICESTER WARREN (Lord De Tabley). Illustrations and Cover Design by C. S. RICKETTS. Second Edition. Crown 8vo. 7s. 6d. net.

DIAL (THE).

No. 1 of the Second Series. Illustrations by RICKETTS, SHANNON, PISSARRO. 200 only. 4to. £1, 1s. net.
[Very few remain.
The present series will be continued at irregular intervals.

EGERTON (GEORGE).

KEYNOTES : Short Stories. With Title-page by AUBREY
BEARDSLEY. Second Edition. Crown 8vo. 3s. 6d.
net.

FIELD (MICHAEL).

SIGHT AND SONG. (Poems on Pictures.) 400 copies.
Fcap. 8vo. 5s. net.   [*Very few remain.*

FIELD (MICHAEL).

STEPHANIA : A Trialogue in Three Acts. 250 copies.
Pott 4to. 6s. net.   [*Very few remain.*

GALE (NORMAN).

ORCHARD SONGS. Fcap. 8vo. With Title-page and
Cover Design by J. ILLINGWORTH KAY. 5s. net.

Also a Special Edition limited in number on hand-made paper
bound in English vellum. £1, 1s. net.

GARNETT (RICHARD).

A VOLUME OF POEMS. 350 copies. Crown 8vo. With
Title-page designed by J. ILLINGWORTH KAY. 5s. net.

GOSSE (EDMUND).

THE LETTERS OF THOMAS LOVELL BEDDOES. Now
first edited. Pott 8vo. 5s. net.

[*Immediately.*

GRAHAME (KENNETH).

PAGAN PAPERS : A Volume of Essays. Fcap. 8vo.
5s. net.

GREENE (G. A.).

ITALIAN LYRISTS OF TO-DAY. Translations in the
original metres from about thirty-five living Italian
poets, with bibliographical and biographical notes.
Crown 8vo. 5s. net.

HAKE (DR. T. GORDON).

A SELECTION FROM HIS POEMS. Edited by Mrs. MEYNELL. With a Portrait after D. G. ROSSETTI. Crown 8vo. 5s. net. [*Immediately*.

HALLAM (ARTHUR HENRY).

THE POEMS, together with his essay 'On Some of the Characteristics of Modern Poetry and on the Lyrical Poems of ALFRED TENNYSON.' Edited, with an Introduction, by RICHARD LE GALLIENNE. 550 copies. Fcap. 8vo. 5s. net. [*Very few remain.*

HAMILTON (COL. IAN).

THE BALLAD OF HADJI AND OTHER POEMS. Etched Frontispiece by WM. STRANG. 50 copies. Fcap. 8vo. 3s. net.
Transferred by the Author to the present Publishers.

HAYES (ALFRED).

THE VALE OF ARDEN AND OTHER POEMS. With Title-page and Cover Design by LAURENCE HOUSMAN. Fcap. 8vo. 5s. net. [*In preparation.*

HICKEY (EMILY H.).

VERSE TALES, LYRICS AND TRANSLATIONS. 300 copies. Imp. 16mo. 5s. net.

HORNE (HERBERT P.).

DIVERSI COLORES : Poems. With ornaments by the Author. 250 copies. 16mo. 5s. net.

IMAGE (SELWYN).

CAROLS AND POEMS. With decorations by H. P. HORNE. 250 copies. 16mo. 5s. net. [*In preparation.*

JAMES (W. P.).

ROMANTIC PROFESSIONS : A Volume of Essays, with Title-page by J. ILLINGWORTH KAY. Crown 8vo. 5s. net.
[*Immediately.*

JOHNSON (EFFIE).

IN THE FIRE AND OTHER FANCIES. Frontispiece by WALTER CRANE. 500 copies. Imp. 16mo. 3s. 6d. net.

JOHNSON (LIONEL).

THE ART OF THOMAS HARDY: Six Essays. With Etched Portrait by WM. STRANG, and Bibliography by JOHN LANE. Crown 8vo. 5s. 6d. net.

Also 150 copies, large paper, with proofs of the portrait. £1, 1s. net. [*Very shortly.*]

JOHNSON (LIONEL).

A VOLUME OF POEMS. Fcap. 8vo. 5s. net.
[*In preparation.*]

KEATS (JOHN).

THREE ESSAYS, now issued in book form for the first time. Edited by H. BUXTON FORMAN. With Life-mask by HAYDON. Fcap. 4to. 10s. 6d. net.
[*Very few remain.*]

LEATHER (R. K.).

VERSES. 250 copies. Fcap. 8vo. 3s. net.

Transferred by the Author to the present Publishers.

LEATHER (R. K.), & RICHARD LE GALLIENNE.

THE STUDENT AND THE BODY-SNATCHER AND OTHER TRIFLES. [*Small paper edition out of print.*] There remain a very few of the 50 large paper copies. 7s. 6d. net.

LE GALLIENNE (RICHARD).

PROSE FANCIES. With a Portrait of the Author. Cr. 8vo. 5s. net.

Also a limited large paper edition. 12s. 6d. net. [*In preparation.*]

LE GALLIENNE (RICHARD).

THE BOOK BILLS OF NARCISSUS. An Account rendered by RICHARD LE GALLIENNE. Second Edition. Crown 8vo, buckram. 3s. 6d. net.

LE GALLIENNE (RICHARD).
ENGLISH POEMS. Third Edition, cr. 8vo. 5s. net.

LE GALLIENNE (RICHARD).
GEORGE MEREDITH: Some Characteristics. With a Bibliography (much enlarged) by JOHN LANE, portrait, etc. Third Edition. Crown 8vo. 5s. 6d. net.

LE GALLIENNE (RICHARD).
THE RELIGION OF A LITERARY MAN. Cr. 8vo. 3rd thousand. 3s. 6d. net.
Also a special rubricated edition on hand-made paper. 8vo. 10s. 6d. net.

LETTERS TO LIVING ARTISTS.
500 copies. Fcap. 8vo. 3s. 6d. net. [Very few remain.

MARSTON (PHILIP BOURKE).
A LAST HARVEST: LYRICS AND SONNETS FROM THE BOOK OF LOVE. Edited by LOUISE CHANDLER MOULTON. 500 copies. Fcap. 8vo. 5s. net.
Also 50 copies on large paper, hand-made. 10s. 6d. net.
[Very few remain.

MARTIN (W. WILSEY).
QUATRAINS, LIFE'S MYSTERY AND OTHER POEMS. 16mo. 2s. 6d. net. [Very few remain.

MARZIALS (THEO.).
THE GALLERY OF PIGEONS AND OTHER POEMS. Fcap. 8vo. 4s. 6d. net. [Very few remain.
Transferred by the Author to the present Publishers.

MEYNELL (MRS.), (ALICE C. THOMPSON).
POEMS. Second Edition. Fcap. 8vo. 3s. 6d. net. A few of the 50 large paper copies (First Edition) remain, 12s. 6d. net.

MEYNELL (MRS.).
> THE RHYTHM OF LIFE, AND OTHER ESSAYS. Second Edition. Fcap. 8vo. 3s. 6d. net. A few of the 50 large paper copies (First Edition) remain. 12s. 6d. net.

MURRAY (ALMA).
> PORTRAIT AS BEATRICE CENCI. With critical notice containing four letters from ROBERT BROWNING. 8vo, wrapper. 2s. net.

NETTLESHIP (J. T.).
> ROBERT BROWNING : Essays and Thoughts. Third Edition. Crown 8vo. 5s. 6d. net. Half a dozen of the Whatman large paper copies (First Edition) remain. £1, 1s. net.

NOBLE (JAS. ASHCROFT).
> THE SONNET IN ENGLAND AND OTHER ESSAYS. Title-page and Cover Design by AUSTIN YOUNG. 600 copies. Crown 8vo. 5s. net.
>
> Also 50 copies large paper. 12s. 6d. net.

NOEL (HON. RODEN).
> POOR PEOPLE'S CHRISTMAS. 250 copies. 16mo. 1s. net.
> [*Very few remain.*

OXFORD CHARACTERS.
> A series of lithographed portraits by WILL ROTHENSTEIN, with text by F. YORK POWELL and others. To be issued monthly in term. Each number will contain two portraits. Part I. contains portraits of SIR HENRY ACLAND and Mr. W. A. L. FLETCHER, and Part II. of Mr. ROBINSON K. ELLIS, and LORD ST. CYRES. 200 copies only, folio, wrapper, 5s. net per part ; 25 special copies containing proof impressions of the portraits signed by the artist, 10s. 6d. net per part.

PINKERTON (PERCY).
> GALEAZZO : A Venetian Episode and other Poems. Etched Frontispiece. 16mo. 5s. net.
> [*Very few remain.*
> *Transferred by the Author to the present Publishers.*

RADFORD (DOLLIE).
>SONGS. A New Volume of Verse. [*In preparation.*

RADFORD (ERNEST).
>CHAMBERS TWAIN. Frontispiece by WALTER CRANE. 250 copies. Imp. 16mo. 5s. net.
>Also 50 copies large paper. 10s. 6d. net. [*Very few remain.*

RHYMERS' CLUB, THE BOOK OF THE.
>A second series is in preparation.

SCHAFF (DR. P.).
>LITERATURE AND POETRY: Papers on Dante, etc. Portrait and Plates, 100 copies only. 8vo. 10s. net.

SCOTT (WM. BELL).
>A POET'S HARVEST HOME: WITH AN AFTERMATH. 300 copies. Fcap. 8vo. 5s. net. [*Very few remain.*
>*.* *Will not be reprinted.*

SHAW (A. D. L.).
>THE HAPPY WANDERER. Poems. Fcap. 8vo. 5s. net.
>[*In preparation.*

STODDARD (R. H.).
>THE LION'S CUB; WITH OTHER VERSE. Portrait. 100 copies only, bound in an illuminated Persian design. Fcap. 8vo. 5s. net. [*Very few remain.*

SYMONDS (JOHN ADDINGTON).
>IN THE KEY OF BLUE, AND OTHER PROSE ESSAYS. Cover designed by C. S. RICKETTS. Second Edition. Thick Crown 8vo. 8s. 6d. net.

THOMPSON (FRANCIS).
>A VOLUME OF POEMS. With Frontispiece, Title-page and Cover Design by LAURENCE HOUSMAN. Second Edition. Pott 4to. 5s. net.

TODHUNTER (JOHN).
>A SICILIAN IDYLL. Frontispiece by WALTER CRANE. 250 copies. Imp. 16mo. 5s. net.
>Also 50 copies large paper, fcap. 4to. 10s. 6d. net.
>[*Very few remain.*

TOMSON (GRAHAM R.).
>AFTER SUNSET. A Volume of Poems. With Title-page and Cover Design by R. ANNING BELL. Fcap. 8vo. 5s. net.
>
>Also a limited large paper edition. 12s. 6d. net. [In preparation.

TREE (H. BEERBOHM).
>THE IMAGINATIVE FACULTY: A Lecture delivered at the Royal Institution. With portrait of Mr. TREE from an unpublished drawing by the Marchioness of Granby. Fcap. 8vo, boards. 2s. 6d. net.

TYNAN HINKSON (KATHARINE).
>CUCKOO SONGS. With Title-page and Cover Design by LAURENCE HOUSMAN. 500 copies. Fcap. 8vo. 5s. net. [In preparation.

VAN DYKE (HENRY).
>THE POETRY OF TENNYSON. Third Edition, enlarged. Crown 8vo. 5s. 6d. net.
>
>*The late Laureate himself gave valuable aid in correcting various details.*

WATSON (WILLIAM).
>THE ELOPING ANGELS: A Caprice. Second Edition. Square 16mo, buckram. 3s. 6d. net.

WATSON (WILLIAM).
>EXCURSIONS IN CRITICISM: being some Prose Recreations of a Rhymer. Second Edition. Cr. 8vo. 5s. net.

WATSON (WILLIAM).
>THE PRINCE'S QUEST, AND OTHER POEMS. With a Bibliographical Note added. Second Edition. Fcap. 8vo. 4s. 6d. net.

WEDMORE (FREDERICK).
>PASTORALS OF FRANCE—RENUNCIATIONS. A volume of Stories. Title-page by JOHN FULLEYLOVE, R.I. Crown 8vo. 5s. net.
>
>*A few of the large paper copies of Renunciations (First Edition) remain. 10s. 6d. net.*

WICKSTEED (P. H.).
 DANTE. Six Sermons. Third Edition. Crown 8vo. 2s. net.
WILDE (OSCAR).
 THE SPHINX. A poem decorated throughout in line and
 colour, and bound in a design by CHARLES RICKETTS.
 250 copies. £2, 2s. net. 25 copies large paper.
 £5, 5s. net. [*Very shortly.*
WILDE (OSCAR).
 The incomparable and ingenious history of Mr. W. H.,
 being the true secret of Shakespear's sonnets now for
 the first time here fully set forth, with initial letters
 and cover design by CHARLES RICKETTS. 500 copies.
 10s. 6d. net.
 Also 50 copies large paper. 21s. net. [*In preparation.*
WILDE (OSCAR).
 DRAMATIC WORKS, now printed for the first time with a
 specially designed Title-page and binding to each
 volume, by CHARLES SHANNON. 500 copies. Small
 4to. 7s. 6d. net per vol.
 Also 50 copies large paper. 15s. net per vol.
 Vol. I. LADY WINDERMERE'S FAN: A Comedy in
  Four Acts. [*Ready.*
 Vol. II. A WOMAN OF NO IMPORTANCE: A Comedy
  in Four Acts. [*Shortly.*
 Vol. III. THE DUCHESS OF PADUA: A Blank Verse
  Tragedy in Five Acts. [*In preparation.*
WILDE (OSCAR).
 SALOMÉ: A Tragedy in one Act, done into English.
 With 11 Illustrations, title-page, and Cover Design
 by AUBREY BEARDSLEY. 500 copies. Small 4to.
 15s. net.
 Also 100 copies, large paper. 30s. net. [*Shortly.*
WYNNE (FRANCES).
 WHISPER. A Volume of Verse. With a Memoir by
 Katharine Tynan and a Portrait added. Fcap. 8vo.
 2s. 6d. net.
 Transferred by the Author to the present Publishers.

The Hobby Horse

A new series of this illustrated magazine will be published quarterly by subscription, under the Editorship of Herbert P. Horne. Subscription £1 per annum, post free, for the four numbers. Quarto, printed on hand-made paper, and issued in a limited edition to subscribers only. The Magazine will contain articles upon Literature, Music, Painting, Sculpture, Architecture, and the Decorative Arts; Poems; Essays; Fiction; original Designs; with reproductions of pictures and drawings by the old masters and contemporary artists. There will be a new title-page and ornaments designed by the Editor. Among the contributors to the Hobby Horse are :

The late MATTHEW ARNOLD.
LAURENCE BINYON.
WILFRID BLUNT.
FORD MADOX BROWN.
The late ARTHUR BURGESS.
E. BURNE-JONES, A.R.A.
AUSTIN DOBSON.
RICHARD GARNETT, LL.D.
A. J. HIPKINS, F.S.A.
SELWYN IMAGE.
LIONEL JOHNSON.
RICHARD LE GALLIENNE.
SIR F. LEIGHTON, Bart., P.R.A.
T. HOPE MCLACHLAN.
MAY MORRIS.
C. HUBERT H. PARRY, Mus. Doc.
A. W. POLLARD.

F. YORK POWELL.
CHRISTINA G. ROSSETTI.
W. M. ROSSETTI.
JOHN RUSKIN, D.C.L., LL.D.
FREDERICK SANDYS.
The late W. BELL SCOTT.
FREDERICK J. SHIELDS.
J. H. SHORTHOUSE.
The late JAMES SMETHAM.
SIMEON SOLOMON.
A. SOMERVELL.
The late J. ADDINGTON SYMONDS.
KATHARINE TYNAN.
G. F. WATTS, R.A.
FREDERICK WEDMORE.
OSCAR WILDE.

Prospectuses on Application.

THE BODLEY HEAD, VIGO STREET, LONDON, W.

'Nearly every book put out by Messrs. Elkin Mathews & John Lane, at the Sign of the Bodley Head, is a satisfaction to the special senses of the modern bookman for bindings, shapes, types, and papers. They have surpassed themselves, and registered a real achievement in English bookmaking by the volume of " Poems, Dramatic and Lyrical," of Lord De Tabley.'

Newcastle Daily Chronicle.

'A ray of hopefulness is stealing again into English poetry after the twilight greys of Clough and Arnold and Tennyson. Even unbelief wears braver colours. Despite the jeremiads, which are the dirges of the elder gods, England is still a nest of singing-birds (*teste* the Catalogue of Elkin Mathews and John Lane).' —Mr. ZANGWILL in *Pall Mall Magazine.*

'All Messrs. Mathews & Lane's Books are so beautifully printed and so tastefully issued, that it rejoices the heart of a book-lover to handle them ; but they have shown their sound judgment not less markedly in the literary quality of their publications. The choiceness of form is not inappropriate to the matter, which is always of something more than ephemeral worth. This was a distinction on which the better publishers at one time prided themselves ; they never lent their names to trash ; but some names associated with worthy traditions have proved more than once a delusion and a snare. The record of Messrs. Elkin Mathews & John Lane is perfect in this respect, and their imprint is a guarantee of the worth of what they publish.'—*Birmingham Daily Post*, Nov. 6, 1893.

'One can nearly always be certain when one sees on the title-page of any given book the name of Messrs Elkin Mathews & John Lane as being the publishers thereof that there will be something worth reading to be found between the boards.'— *World.*

Edinburgh: T. and A. Constable
Printers to Her Majesty